PENGUIN BOOKS

A YEAR IN THE CENTRE

Brian O'Driscoll was born in Dublin in 1979. At twenty-one he scored a hat-trick of tries against France, and at twenty-three he was made captain of Ireland. He was already Ireland's all-time leading try-scorer. In 2001 he was a first-string player on the Lions tour of Australia, and in 2005 he captained the Lions on their tour of New Zealand.

A Year in the Centre

BRIAN O'DRISCOLL

PENGUIN BOOKS

PENGUIN BOOKS

Published by the Penguin Group
Penguin Books Ltd, 80 Strand, London WC2R ORL, England
Penguin Group (USA) Inc., 375 Hudson Street, New York, New York 10014, USA
Penguin Group (Canada), 90 Eglinton Avenue East, Suite 700, Toronto, Ontario, Canada M4P 2Y3
(a division of Pearson Penguin Canada Inc.)
Penguin Ireland, 25 St Stephen's Green, Dublin 2, Ireland
(a division of Penguin Books Ltd)
Penguin Group (Australia), 250 Camberwell Road,
Camberwell, Victoria 3124, Australia (a division of Pearson Australia Group Pty Ltd)
Penguin Books India Pvt Ltd, 11 Community Centre,
Panchsheel Park, New Delhi – 110 017, India
Penguin Group (NZ), cnr Airborne and Rosedale Roads, Albany,
Auckland 1310, New Zealand (a division of Pearson New Zealand Ltd)
Penguin Books (South Africa) (Pty) Ltd, 24 Sturdee Avenue,
Rosebank, Johannesburg 2196, South Africa

Penguin Books Ltd, Registered Offices: 80 Strand, London WC2R ORL, England

www.penguin.com

First published Penguin Ireland 2005
Published in Penguin Books 2006

I

Copyright © Brian O'Driscoll, 2005

All inset photos © Billy Stickland/Inpho, except for the following supplied by author:
2, top, 11, top and bottom, 24, top and bottom

The moral right of the author has been asserted

Typeset by Rowland Phototypesetting Ltd, Bury St Edmunds, Suffolk
Printed in Great Britain by Clays Ltd, St Ives plc

ISBN-13: 978–1–844–88079–9
ISBN-10: 1–844–88079–6

This book is dedicated to the memory of Teddy McShane. His parents, Jim – who has given so much to rugby – and Dolores, are very much in our thoughts.

Contents

Interesting Times

Saturday 11 December 2004, en route to New York

They say flying can do strange things to your mind, and an aeroplane is not the best place to commit thoughts to paper, but what the hell: this little diary of a year in the life of a professional rugby player has to start somewhere, and cruising at 550 mph at 37,000 feet with my feet up seems as good a place as any. I have been nervous about starting it. Is anybody really interested in my life and what I get up to? Then again, I'm always curious as to what pop stars and film stars get up to, and all those reality TV programmes can catch you unawares and you suddenly become hooked. Anyway, I can't put it off any longer. I have the headset on, Guns N' Roses at full blast, and it's time to put up or shut up.

The tantalizing smell of breakfast and freshly brewed coffee is coming from the galley just down the aisle, and I haven't had – haven't been allowed – a full Irish for a good while. Pretty tired – exhausted in fact – but feeling relaxed and pleased with myself, if that doesn't sound too arrogant. Last night I was in Bourgoin, where Leinster sneaked an invaluable win in the Heineken Cup, and now, barely ten hours later, I am mid-Atlantic, on a little pre-Christmas jolly guaranteed to lift the spirits. Flew back on the team charter, arrived about 3 a.m. and booked myself into the Great Southern Hotel at Dublin airport for a couple of hours' sleep – actually I don't think I slept a wink, what with the adrenalin still pumping and one ear cocked for my wake-up call – and then dashed for the 8.30 a.m. flight to New York. All very rock 'n' roll, and why not? I've been living like a monk for the past couple of months. It is time to let off steam. There was a great feeling of freedom when we took off and headed west a couple of hours ago; I was almost lightheaded and couldn't stop smiling to myself.

Best of all, hardly anybody knows what I am up to. That's probably just as well, because sections of the media are convinced I drink and party too much and spend too much time on 'extracurricular activities', whatever that means. Is getting on with a normal life classified as 'extracurricular' these days? Apparently it is in some quarters. For the record I would say I drink considerably less than most 25-year-old single male Dubliners, but I am a big believer in the occasional session with family or friends. I am from the 'work hard, play hard' school and that's exactly what I intend doing now. I've worked my butt off over the last three or four months, in fact ever since we started pre-season in the summer, and I've earned a little down-time.

So it's the Big Apple, followed by a few days' R and R on the Caribbean Island of St Barth's, a Christmas treat to myself after a pretty brutal autumn at rugby's coalface. Then it will be back home for a relaxing family Christmas with all the traditional trimmings, which I love. From the New Year onwards it will be flat out all the way – Heineken Cup, Six Nations and hopefully the Lions in New Zealand – so now is definitely the time to make merry.

Travelling light and on my own since splitting up with my girlfriend Glenda a while back. The Irish press have been full of the whys and wherefores but we have both decided to keep quiet. There's not that much to tell anyway. It's all pretty amicable and it might well just be a temporary thing because basically we are mad about each other. It must be hell going out with a twenty-five-year-old professional rugby player. The last year has been a mad time and the next six or seven months aren't going to see any let-up on the travelling.

New York is one of my very favourite cities – 24/7 fun and entertainment, which is exactly what I am looking for at the moment. It's not a rugby city, and, unlike in Dublin, nobody knows me from Adam, so I can hang out where I want, do what I want and generally just get lost among its 11 or 12 million inhabitants.

This journal should be a bit of fun if nothing else. Being realistic, I will not be making daily entries but I will try to record my thoughts whenever I have a bit of time. It will probably be a bit like a match, all very routine for a while with nothing much happening, and then mayhem. This could be some year . . . or I could break a leg in my next game for Leinster and it will all end in tears. Let's try to be positive, though. Leinster have big hopes in the Heineken Cup, Ireland definitely have a shot at the Grand Slam and a Lions tour to New Zealand is a once-in-a-lifetime experience I do not want to miss out on. There is even talk of me captaining the Lions if my form and fitness hold up. Do I want it? Of course. I would absolutely love to captain the Lions, there is no bigger honour in the game. It's a huge motivation for me. Like every other player who has got any sense I will try to deflect all the questions and hype about the Lions until I know I'm definitely on the plane to Auckland, in whatever capacity, but it will be in the background all the time over the coming months. How could it be otherwise?

Tuesday 14 December, St Barth's, West Indies

Air temperature: 32 degrees. Water temperature: 27 degrees. Forecast: partly cloudy. Atmosphere: chilled. Factor 30 on. Wow, that was a weekend and a half. Where did that come from? Must have been brewing for a good while. Sweet Jesus, do I feel tired, but happy and chilled. Been sleeping around the clock since arriving here in paradise. Well, that's a slight fib. I surface occasionally for food and a swim and to take in the daily fashion parade on the beach – seriously, they have a catwalk and an announcer, the works. There are also loads of fashion shoots on the beach with some of the world's most beautiful women. It's hellish here. God knows how we are going to survive five days of this. Its getting very hot, so time to retire to my sunlounger in the shade – my Irish complexion isn't great for tanning – and listen to a few sounds. My ribs are still sore, not from Bourgoin, but from all the laughing in New York.

New York was a blast. Met up with my buddy Damien – aka Damo, an old mate from Clontarf – and his brother Matt. They were installed in the lap of luxury, staying at the beautiful Chelsea apartment of Vanessa Whelan, daughter of Bill of *Riverdance* fame. The previous twenty-four hours were beginning to catch up with me, and initially I promised myself just a couple of quiet beers before hitting the town big-time on Sunday. When I arrived the boys were out – after a couple of very heavy nights they had decided they ought to get some essentials in such as food, tea bags and milk – and I just lazed around chatting with Nessa, whom I had not met before. She was very cool and great company. We talked about all sorts before the lads arrived back with Zoe Jordan, daughter of

Eddie of Formula 1 fame, and the plan for the night. You always need a plan when aiming for a big night. Apparently we were going to start at the Brass Monkey and then move on to a hot new nightclub called Marquee.

That was fine by me. Brass Monkey is a cosy Irish pub that hasn't strayed over the top into a themed Irish bar. The owner, Shaun Cunningham, who runs another bar near by, is an old friend and he has a great oppo called Joe. To my shame I can't remember his surname – he is listed as 'Joe New York' in my mobile phone and I guess that's what he will always be now. They are a great double act, very entertaining.

Loads of banter at Brass Monkey and not a word about rugby, I am glad to say. Then we moved on to the club, and what a scene that was, a real exclusive celebrity haunt, famed apparently for being where all the catwalk models go to dance and be seen. Colin Farrell is also a regular, and among the celebrities it now seemed you would have to number Damo and Matt, who were on first-name terms with the bouncers and barmen, having undertaken extensive research on my behalf before I arrived. They were posing around like Puff Daddy and obviously to the manner born. We were ushered in past a long queue of beautiful people and soon found ourselves sitting on the plushest white leather couches money can buy, perfectly stationed between the bar and dance floor. We had a table booked and a steady procession of people promenaded by, checking us out, just in case we were famous – very amusing. Nobody recognized us. There was an amazing chandelier over the dance floor that changed colour with the music that was all very technomix. I wouldn't have batted an eyelid if John Travolta had appeared on the dance floor and strutted his stuff. A very long night ensued, and I was the last one left standing, ordering the taxi and getting the others home.

Despite sticking to my usual Corona – I find I don't get too wasted or obnoxious on it when the big session is on – I felt pretty shabby the next morning, sorry, lunchtime, when I woke up. Everybody else was still stoked and wanted to bat on, so who was I to spoil the party? The session had not run its course yet by any means. We had a fabulous lunch at some restaurant where they filmed *Sex and the City*, then nipped into the Brass Monkey about 4 p.m., just for the one. Bad mistake. We were all hitting our stride now and intent on putting the world to rights. I laughed till I nearly cried and felt all the tension of the previous couple of months slipping away. It was a very Irish sort of gathering, all of us taking it in turns to tell our little stories. We crashed on very late – God, what happened then? Give us a minute while I try to piece this together. That's right, Matt went home about midnight – he was sensible and had a flight back to Dublin the next morning – but the rest of us hit the club again and got back just before breakfast time, fully intending to grab an hour's sleep before heading for the airport and the sunny Caribbean. Of course we overslept and missed our connection and Damo had to spend a couple of hours on the phone fast talking – and there is no one faster or more persuasive in these situations – before we got on the late-afternoon flight. We arrived last night totally pickled, and I went straight to bed. Session officially over. Thankfully.

Wednesday 15 December, St Barth's

Air temperature: 31 degrees. Water temperature: 27 degrees. Forecast: partly cloudy. Atmosphere: idyllic. Sunblock: factor 30. Detox under way. Refreshing swim, sunblock on, light lunch of salad ordered, iced water by my side, sounds playing gently in the background. Classic U2 stuff. Looking OK-ish but feeling a bit self-conscious in my designer shades. My style is more designer grunge than cool dude. Still feeling a bit jaded to be honest. The abuse we put our bodies through, one way or another. What the hell. You are only young once and I deserve a holiday as much as the next man. That's what I keep telling myself, anyway.

Right, today I am going to have a serious look at what's been going on in my rugby life for the last two or three months and attempt to put it all in perspective, a sort of mental cleaning of the tubes. Sometimes in this game you are so busy that you don't get a chance to review and reflect and maybe glimpse the bigger picture. So this should be a good exercise.

First up, the autumn internationals, and that means South Africa. They arrived as the reigning Tri-Nations champions and off the back of a pretty impressive win over Wales at the Millennium Stadium. Our preparation was perfect. Everybody was hungry and focused and everything went smoothly. We were damned near faultless on the training pitch, the video analysis from Mervyn Murphy was spot on. Felt sharp as a needle. I have never known a fortnight to match it.

We didn't need their coach Jake White's barbed comments to gee us up – he reckoned only two or three of our team would make the Boks' starting XV and that there was no way South Africa could lose – because we could not have been more motivated. I wasn't at all happy with the way we had performed in South Africa in the summer. We went down there as Triple Crown champions but we just didn't perform. OK, the matches looked close enough and we did have our moments, but we didn't threaten them and after our great wins over England, France and Australia in the recent past I had hoped for much more. Perhaps we were just tired, but it was definitely a backwards step. To be honest, I was pretty narked about it, so was the squad, and our coach, Eddie O'Sullivan, was really fed up. We were in danger of undoing a lot of good work if we weren't able to step up this autumn.

Back in Ireland Eddie immediately decreed that we needed to bulk up, and putting the pounds on was the emphasis of our pre-season training. We deliberately put on weight in the sure knowledge that in the ten-month season ahead there would be plenty of opportunity to trim down. It's the same theory as a horse carrying a few extra pounds in the first race of the season. It wasn't rocket science, just plain common sense. The provinces didn't like it because it meant we all made a delayed start to the domestic season, but sometimes the national need comes first. Eddie fought the political battles, and we kept heading down the gym and eating for Ireland. Contrary to what one or two commentators were suggesting I wasn't putting on the extra weight by upping my booze intake – quite the contrary, actually, if only they knew. As we beasted ourselves I went the whole hog health-wise and gave up drink for the entire ten weeks of the pre-season. Didn't enjoy it at all, didn't feel any better for it, did not relax and sleep as well as I usually do. Won't be doing that again in a hurry.

The South Africa game was one of our very best perform-ances – in fact our best, in my opinion – and it now means that New Zealand is the only side in the world this current Irish crop has never beaten. We have knocked the big sides off one by one, and every time I feel our game has grown a little.

South Africa arrived full of themselves and cocky. Yes, they had beaten us well in the summer and then nicked a very even Tri-Nations tournament, but we always thought they were very beatable. I had assumed the normal fickle Dublin weather would at least lend a hand – in fact I remember telling the Boks to bring their wellies in one of my post-Test captain's speeches in the summer – but come 13 November it was a perfect late autumn day at Lansdowne Road, ideal for whatever brand of rugby you chose. We put in a very physical effort up front but the match really belonged to Ronan O'Gara – he was absolutely superb, probably his best performance in an Ireland shirt. ROG was in the zone right from the off and just took control of everything as well as poaching that cheeky try from the tapped penalty.

Then came the USA the following week. Some were surprised that a fair few of the senior players started this game, but they misunderstood what motivates an international sportsman. You always want to play, you always want to collect caps, score tries and – if we are being honest – keep the contenders for our places out of contention. Also, when you are captain of your country it all gets very addictive. The chance to run on to Lansdowne Road in the green shirt is not something I would ever give up lightly.

Having said all that, I was definitely hoping to slope off shortly after half-time with a view to the Argentina game and looked hopefully over to the bench, but Eddie and the management seemed to forget our pre-match plan and opted to keep me going much longer! Perhaps they thought I needed the fitness work. Anyway, it didn't matter, it was enjoyable to see a couple of the new lads like Tommy Bowe and Denis Leamy get a run and integrate into the squad. We played some very decent stuff against a physical and fit side, although the States were pretty limited in attack and didn't pose much threat.

Thursday 16 December, St Barth's

Air temperature: 30 degrees. Water temperature: 27 degrees. Forecast: partly cloudy. Atmosphere: reflective. Sunblock: factor 24. Fresh pineapple and guava juice for breakfast. Feeling fantastic, even tried to learn the butterfly in the swimming pool. How do they do that? I'm in a Bruce Springsteen mood and he's playing away in the background. Fresh grilled fish for lunch. The food here is amazing, as you would expect from a little colonial corner of France.

Might even be a complete muppet this evening and do an hour in the gym, I'm feeling that good. But then again I might just go for a walk and a snorkel off the hotel beach. There are fourteen beaches on the island, apparently, all within about ten minutes' drive. It's very laid back here. Even the official tourist guide admits there isn't much to do in the capital, Gustavia – it used to be Swedish before the French took over – except to relax and enjoy the world-class dining. That's where I come in.

Didn't finish my debrief yesterday due to the fact that I fell asleep on my lounger and it was dark when I woke up. Or maybe I was just putting off the worst bit. Didn't enjoy the Argentina match at all. One of the lowlights of my international career, for various reasons. OK, there was a certain satisfaction in somehow manufacturing a win when we had played so poorly, but that was the sum of it.

Firstly, hands up, it was a poor performance from Ireland and we were fortunate to escape with a win. We have played much better than that and lost. It was very subdued in the dressing room afterwards. We were all pretty depressed and fed up with the Pumas' tactics. Six of us came in for the treatment at various times in the game and needed medical attention to our eyes and surrounding areas. I can assure you it is not very pleasant. Eddie was livid. I went to hospital the next morning to get a painful scratch on my eye sorted out; luckily it just needed a course of eye-drops.

As captain I felt duty-bound to point out to referee Tony Spreadbury what was going on, especially after one obvious attack on ROG, but I am not sure the message got home. In fairness it's a very difficult thing to spot and legislate on. A referee's nightmare. It all goes on deep in the rucks and mauls where nothing much can be seen.

Don't ask me why they do it. It has no part in rugby and they are out of order. There's a bit of me which says: 'Sod it, if you want to win so badly that you are prepared to maim and blind an opponent, here, have the bloody victory.' And there is a bigger part of me which says, 'No way will I let you win using these tactics.' The best way to put a cheat in his place is by consistently beating him.

Pretty disappointed in the Pumas because we in Ireland know better than most what a fine rugby team they can be, and are. I appreciate they get a rough deal on the world scene and probably get very frustrated at times, but come on, guys, that's not the way. You are good enough to take major Test scalps on your rugby skills alone. Do that consistently and perhaps you will get a warmer welcome from the international rugby community.

Felipe Contepomi at Leinster, who was playing fly-half for the Pumas, is one of the nicest blokes you will ever meet – erudite, trainee doctor and a true gent. There's no way he would ever get involved in that stuff, and I've been too embarrassed to ask him about it ever since. He is first and foremost a Leinster colleague and a good mate but perhaps one day I should. I can't get my head around it at all.

It took a while to click into party mode that night, but eventually we all regained our good spirits and reflected on a bloody hard month in camp. Three matches, three wins, two of them excellent, one lucky and ultimately unsatisfactory. All in all it was a pretty useful autumn, but I wasn't entirely happy. It worried me that we failed to produce a better performance against Argentina. Sure, they are a good side and we allowed ourselves to become distracted, but Ireland should be good enough now to dispatch that kind of team, especially at Lansdowne Road. Back home we had stocked up in preparation for a party, and much later that night a whole platoon of the guys arrived back for the session, just good ad hoc fun, banter and a couple of songs. My elder sister, Jules, had just announced her engagement to Tomás Kennedy, so there is definitely something for the O'Driscoll clan to get excited about. You don't have to be hitting the nightclubs and late bars to be having a good time; sometimes you just want to be at home with your mates and family.

Friday 17 December, St Barth's

Air temperature: 32 degrees. Water temperature: 28 degrees. Forecast: clear. Atmosphere: mellow. Another bloody day in paradise! Been a superb break, even got the hint of a tan. Had a couple of beers last night, but just a couple, a sort of concession to still being on holiday, but nothing manic. Feeling fantastic and want to keep it that way.

Nearly finished with my debrief. Very conscious I haven't mentioned Leinster yet. They are the cornerstone of my rugby life, it's just that the international scene takes over at certain times of the year.

Leinster so far have been good. We have been disappointed at missing the boat a couple of times in the Heineken Cup in recent years, especially a shocking semi-final against Perpignan at Lansdowne Road two years ago when we just didn't get out of the blocks at all. We stand a decent chance this year. No one side is a clear favourite. Munster are good but no better than before; Leicester didn't go well last year but are returning to form and Martin Johnson will be looking to finish his career on a high. Toulouse are very good in patches but not unbeatable; Biarritz have stacks of potential but go AWOL occasionally. Leinster? Dangerous backs, perhaps a little vulnerable up front, so we need to put our chances away ruthlessly to stay ahead of the game. A sporting chance.

Our first two games came in the lead-up to the autumn internationals. Treviso away was tougher than expected: the Italians were quite a handful before we pulled through 25–9. Nice trip. Treviso is a lovely walled town and it felt very mellow walking around on the Friday, diving into little cafés for a caffè latte or cappuccino. We hardly ever stay after a game these days, so if you are to take in the European experience you have to go for a little wander the day before. We were only forty minutes' drive from Venice, but that was just a little too far and time-consuming. We were there to play rugby, after all.

Then we fronted up to Bath at home. Good win, because the Bath pack is formidable and they have some big names in their back division. It was all pretty tight heading for half-time, with us just 10–8 up and having to defend for our lives. A Bath try then and we could have been in serious trouble, but we held on and ran out for a comfortable 30–11 victory.

A big confidence booster, although Gordon D'Arcy picked up a nasty groin injury which put him out of the autumn internationals.

The doubleheader against Bourgoin was just bizarre. They are blazing a trail in the French championship but put out just four first-teamers in Dublin, and we crucified them 92–17, scoring twelve tries, Shane Horgan leading the way with a hat-trick. We actually played exceptionally well and would have damaged much better teams than Bourgoin Extras that night, but it left a bad taste, and I would have to say the spectators got poor value for money. I am mystified as to why Bourgoin treat the competition in such a cavalier fashion. There are plenty of other teams around Europe that would kill to be in the Heineken Cup.

And then the return last week was full-on, and we escaped by the skin of our teeth. They paraded all their troops in Bourgoin, and they have a beefy pack when they set to work. We hung on and nicked it with three minutes to go when I got over for my second try of the night. Very pleased with that score. It was one of those heightened moments when I felt I was going to get over well before the pass came. The adrenalin was surging, the team needed the try now, it was probably our last chance. Some of the boys said it was almost a carbon copy of the one I got for the Lions in the first Test in 2001. It did feel similar. On both occasions I was pretty sure nothing would stop me. No wonder I was in such good form heading for New York the next morning.

Wednesday 22 December, Dublin

Air temperature: 4 degrees. Cloud cover: total. Forecast: rain and lots of it. Atmosphere: Christmas is coming. Good to be back home, in fact great to be back home. Batteries recharged and a Dublin Christmas to look forward to, not to mention a couple of big Celtic League matches against Ulster, which I don't know if I'll be involved in, and Munster, which is developing into a big grudge match. Both of us are likely to be at full strength for the first time in a long while so this time it will really count.

But first Christmas, which is definitely a time for family and friends as far as I'm concerned. I love all the traditional stuff, especially the Christmas Eve meeting down our local, which is my favourite night of the year, way out ahead of New Year's Eve, which can be a damp squib, and you've had enough by then anyway. Will be taking it fairly easy this year with the Leinster game coming up, but I intend observing the niceties and catching up with everybody.

I am incredibly lucky with my family and friends, a wonderfully normal and loving home life with good people who stick by me. My dad, Frank, is a complete star and a big influence in my life. You can sometimes hear him before you see him: he will be the one cracking the jokes, making the wisecracks, trying to have the last word in a debate and roaring loudest in support on the touchline. I swear to God I can occasionally pick out his particular shout amidst the bedlam of Lansdowne Road on big match days. It takes me back to Blackrock College, with Dad going nuts on the touchline. Mum and my sisters spend a good deal of their time trying to keep him cool, or, if that fails, looking the other way. He lives every match in the moment. Mentally he is out there playing alongside me for the full eighty minutes.

He is an extrovert and enthusiast for life but also a smart-thinking guy and completely unflappable. You won't ever see him fazed or taken aback by anything. He is a GP of thirty years' standing, and there is not much in this world he hasn't seen and coped with, and he is very calm and at his best when there is work to do. If I have inherited one characteristic from Dad, certainly on the rugby field, it is that I normally perform at my best when the pressure is greatest.

That's interesting, actually, thinking back, because at Blackrock College it was the big intense matches and pressure games and all the stomach churning beforehand and foot stomping in the changing rooms that I didn't care for much. That was one season I sort of rebelled for a while and played for Clontarf RFC U16, just for the craic. But then I must have undergone a personality change, or simply matured as a person, because I suddenly realized that it was overcoming your nerves and playing well – in fact playing your best – in the big games that was the best fun of all.

Dad was a very decent centre in his day, a mad kamikaze tackler with a good step and plenty of wheels. That's what all his contemporaries tell me. He toured Argentina with Ireland in the 1970s and played in the 'Tests' – but the IRFU in their wisdom did not award caps against the Pumas in those days, and that was the nearest he ever got to a full international. Of course he sometimes goes at least two hours without somebody mentioning that fact! I guess he was un-lucky as well. With the great Mike Gibson around, one of the two centre berths was most certainly not up for grabs.

Dad is a great friend and in recent years has become a

mentor as well. About three years ago he started overseeing all my commercial affairs, and it was a great weight off my shoulders to be looked after by somebody I could trust completely and with whom I could always immediately talk something through. He works part-time now in the medical practice and probably devotes two days a week to my affairs, for which I shall be eternally grateful.

Mum – Geraldine – is a saint, the voice of reason and sanity, who keeps Dad and the rest of us in order. If Frank is the extrovert joker, Mum is the quiet power behind the throne. They complement each other brilliantly and have been a fantastic couple ever since they met as medical students. Mum is a GP as well, and in the past five years, with the kids all grown up, they have been able to reap the benefits and travel a bit and enjoy more time together.

Most Irish lads love their mammy, and as the only son I am probably doubly blessed. We are very close. I will talk to her about anything, including some pretty personal stuff: she's a real confidante, and we are very happy in each other's company. She helps out with a lot of things in my rugby career as well. She organizes answering all the letters and autograph requests and jerseys to be signed for charity auctions and keeps my life in order when I am away in training camp, trying to concentrate on the rugby. My sisters reckon she pampers me too much, and they are probably right. She is a gem and spoils me rotten, and I wouldn't have it any other way.

My elder sister, Jules, who is thirty-one and a nurse, has now set the wedding date for August, so making sure that all goes off without a hitch is by far the most important thing in the family next year. My other sister, Sue, who is two years younger, works in event management and does a little radio work as well. They were both keen hockey players and like to keep fit in the gym, but otherwise they are not particularly sports-mad. Sue is like Dad, extrovert and confident; Jules is more like Mum and me, a little more laid back and retiring, although confident in what she does.

My sisters are both fantastic; they looked out for me when I was younger without doing the 'big sister' bit. I am very proud of them and close to all my family. They keep me grounded, don't take any nonsense or bullshitting from me if I start acting the big-shot. Nothing ever changes at home; it is where I am most comfortable and can be myself.

Christmas Eve, Dublin

Cold today. Trained with Leinster this morning. Getting ready to hook up with a few of the lads for a jar, probably down at the Dollymount. My friends, like family, are priceless. Firstly there is Barry Toomey – Tombstone to his mates, of whom there are many – my housemate at number 35. We both ended up doing a sports management course in UCD and just hit it off there from day one. We played rugby together there, and discovered that we had actually played against each other for a couple of years when Blackrock met Castleknock.

We get on brilliantly. He is very witty, extremely entertaining and always in good form. He has me in tears laughing at his antics after a long day's training or when I get back from an international trip. We are the odd couple. Eat your hearts out, Jack Lemmon and Walter Matthau. He is a top mate, I would trust him with my life.

Ciaran Scally is another very close friend. Ciaran was a belting scrum-half and was blazing a trail right to the top when he picked up a serious knee injury and was forced out of the game three or four years ago. He had just made it into the Ireland team and, believe me, he was going places. As good a schoolboy player as I can remember. Mick Quinlan is another Blackrock mucker – his brother Dave is a strapping centre in the Leinster squad with me.

Then there is the 'Clontarf set', headed up by Donovan Rossi, who played Ireland U19 with me, and Damien O'Donahue – Damo – and his brother Matt, the now infamous lounge lizards of New York, whom you have already met. True friends who have known me for ever, guys who know the real Brian O'Driscoll, warts and all.

I get on very well with all the Ireland squad, of course, which is just as well since we spend large chunks of our lives together. We live in each other's pockets for much of the year, share the same days off and holidays and have been through so much together that it's probably inevitable that much of my social life centres around them, especially those who, like me, play for Leinster as well.

Christmas Day, Dublin

Vegging for Ireland back home with the folks. Great day yesterday. Couple of quiet ones with friends in the afternoon and then 7 o'clock Mass with the family before they dropped me off at the pub, where I spent most of the evening catching up with old friends. It was last orders at midnight, so as ever I dropped in at the Rossis', a couple of houses down the road, for a few turkey sandwiches. Five or six years ago we called in and were famished after a big night and damn near polished off his mum's Christmas turkey. She has got wise to that now, so she either waits up for us and makes us a tray of sandwiches or leaves a note saying they are in the fridge. Anything to save her family lunch. She would miss us if we didn't turn up one year, though.

New Year's Eve, Cork

Down in Cork for the Munster match tomorrow. My Auntie Gillian and her family live just over the road from the team hotel, and most of the family, including Granny and Mum and Dad, are over with her, so I went over about 11.30 to say hi to everybody and count the New Year down. Then straight back to the hotel to wish my roommate, Shane Horgan, the best. Shaggy is normally a gas character but with a game tomorrow and his style distinctly cramped he has opted for a complete night in, hasn't moved from our room. He's half asleep and just grunts a sort of Happy New Year. It is now 12.17 a.m. Time for bed. Welcome to 2005. God only knows what lies in store this year, but it won't be boring, that's for sure.

Saturday 1 January 2005, Cork

Air temperature: 5 degrees. Forecast: big year ahead. Atmosphere: subdued. Normally I make a resolution every New Year's Day to go on the dry until my birthday on 21 January, but it did me no good whatsoever back in the summer, so I'm binning that idea. Also made a mental note to train with more focus and intensity for the next seven months and offered a little prayer about staying healthy and injury-free.

Just lost out to Munster in a pretty fiery game at Musgrave Park this evening. With the Six Nations so close and with the sides at full strength it amounted to an old-fashioned final Ireland trial. Lots of points to be proved and a few old scores to be settled. Pretty torrid going up front, as you would expect. Hate losing to Munster. Not a great start to 2005.

Tuesday 4 January, number 35, Dublin

Sir Clive Woodward's Power of Four Lions Christmas card and the Lance Armstrong-style wristband finally plop on to the mat. A couple of the guys had mentioned they had got the cards over the holiday – with their message about how the combined power of the four unions can beat the mighty All Blacks – so I was just beginning to wonder why I didn't appear to be on the Christmas list. Sitting in my kitchen enjoying a coffee watching the Sky News, which is unusual for me. Normally I switch straight to MTV or one of the music channels. Now that I'm nearly twenty-six, and a proper adult, I'm trying to take more interest in the big wide world out there. Doesn't come naturally, but getting there.

Sunday 9 January, number 35

Well, Leinster have now used their 'get out of jail free' card for the Heineken this season. We won 27–23 at Bath yesterday, but were trailing 23–13 with four minutes to go after being stuffed out of sight all second half. We hung in well, though, and nicked it through late tries from David Holwell and Malcolm O'Kelly. Their pack beasted us in the tight, and it's a big worry if we are going to go much further in this competition.

We have to be more ruthless. We started well, went 13–3 up and should have walked in a second try under the posts to make it 20–3, but I threw a sloppy pass to Girvan Dempsey and the chance went begging. Life would have been much more comfortable if we could have scored a seven-pointer then, but we didn't. Still, we are the first team to be certain of qualifying and we can make it six out of six next week against Treviso. Not many sides, even the likes of Toulouse and Leicester, have done that. Actually we did once before, two years ago, not that it did us much good. It all ended in tears with a no-show by us in the semi-final against Perpignan.

Friday 21 January, Clontarf, Dublin

My birthday: twenty-six today. Quiet day. Just called in to see the folks. One of Ireland's sponsors, O_2, have given me a specially produced state-of-the-art iPod as a present. It stores either 15,000 or 50,000 tracks, can't remember which. Enough to be getting on with anyway! Have had the long 'blond' locks cut off and opted for a military-style short-back-and-sides haircut. Um, not quite sure about it yet. Seemed like a good idea.

Sunday 23 January, City West, Dublin

Air temperature: 3 degrees. Forecast: the hard work starts now. Atmosphere: excited. The Six Nations build-up has started in earnest and we are back in camp at City West.

Initially I always enjoy the comfort and the fact that everything is laid on and you can get through a mountain of work and preparation with the minimum of hassle, but by the middle of March it will be driving me completely insane, and I will be looking to break out. You can feel imprisoned and institutionalized, at least I do. Your day is mapped out to the final minute. Eat, train, sleep. Eat, train, sleep. You start losing the ability to think and act independently, and I'm not sure how good that is for a sportsman who forges his reputation by thinking and acting independently. Perhaps it doesn't matter too much. I wouldn't do things an awful lot differently at home – training, sleeping, watching music videos, nattering to friends on the mobile – but I would be at home. That's the point, I suppose. Some of the international sides back in the seventies seemed to produce some stunning rugby on the back of two days together maximum. Makes you think, doesn't it?

Struggling a bit with my left shoulder at the moment, more than I really care to admit so close to the Championship, but I've learned not to stress out over injuries. It's an old war wound and it comes and goes. It's nerve damage, and I get the occasional 'stinger' down my arm. I suppose it has the potential to be really troublesome, like Jonny's shoulder.

God, I hope it doesn't come to that. What a nightmare he has had, and now he's gone down with a knee ligament injury during Newcastle's Heineken match in Perpignan. It never rains but it pours. I've liked Jonny ever since we toured Australia with the 2001 Lions – we hit it off right from the start. In fact I've known him even longer than that – we lined up on opposite sides for Ireland and England Schools in 1997. I fancied myself as a goalkicker in those days, but you could see straight away he was a different class.

We have a fair bit in common, although he has become a much bigger fish in an even bigger pond, especially since the World Cup. We are the same age and have faced similar problems getting to grips with what people term stardom and fame. Interesting that in the end we have both turned to our dads to help manage our affairs and all the commercial offers thrown at you. You need somebody you can trust totally. That doesn't necessarily mean that mistakes won't be made, but they will always be honest mistakes.

Anyway, in my own mind I don't think my shoulder is anywhere near as serious as that but it has definitely hindered some of my training over the last couple of weeks. After a session I have to walk around with one of these electro-magnetic TENS pain-relief gadgets strapped to the shoulder – I believe they originally invented them for women in labour. It helps a bit, certainly does no harm.

It's not ideal, though. I'm not exactly where I want to be in terms of preparation going into the Six Nations, but I'm not in bad shape either. There will be plenty of lads with the other Six Nations sides suffering in exactly the same way as I write these very words. Nobody escapes without some pain along the way these days. With that comforting thought it's time for bed.

Monday 24 January, City West

Training and treatment for my shoulder at City West. Can't take a full part in the contact stuff and a bit limited in the gym. Keeping calm, though. Worrying and panicking about injuries does no good whatsoever. And let's be honest here, we are talking sport, not life and death. Those terrible pictures from the Far East after the tsunami disaster on Stephen's Day put a lot of things in perspective for a lot of people. Did a photo-shoot with O_2 in the afternoon and a couple of press interviews this evening. So far so good. Feeling optimistic and excited about the months ahead. The shoot was good fun and the interviews went well, good questions which helped focus my thoughts a little bit.

Tuesday 25 January, City West

Training and treatment in the morning. A photo-shoot with RTE and a big interview with BBC World at lunchtime. Media interviews and photo-shoots have become part of my life and after a slow start – I am pretty shy in a sort of smiley-extrovert-don't-come-too-close sort of way – I have actually grown to almost enjoy them. They break the days and weeks up: life as a rugby professional has its massive highs, but there are some pretty tedious middling weeks in between.

Some of the journos are interesting guys with different takes on things and they usually have all the gossip on other sides and players, and I now really enjoy going into the studio and watching expert photographers and make-up people go to work. Most of us are people-watchers on the quiet and there is always something to be gained by observing somebody who really knows what they are doing. Close contact with excellence, in any form, is always inspiring.

And it's a bit of fun as well. I used to be nervous and self-conscious going into photo-shoots – I suppose I'm an OK-looking guy but definitely no oil painting and used to hate seeing happy snaps of myself, let alone billboard posters in the middle of Dublin and magazine front pages. But now I've learned to relax and take everything in my stride.

You can't take any of the celebrity stuff too seriously. A couple of years back I was 'voted' sexiest male in Ireland, which caused a bit of a fuss. C'mon, guys, get real, it was just a bit of a laugh. Mum loves me and my sisters will stick up for me, but really that is a complete joke. If it was a serious award the Colin Farrells of this world would be getting it year in, year out. Anyway, something that was meant to be pure fun ended up with me getting a load of negative publicity. I was absolutely delighted when I unexpectedly plunged out of the top fifty last year, a washed-up former sex symbol whose time has been and gone.

The BBC World interview was good, a slightly different tone and approach and obviously a different audience. Some – most? – of the viewers presumably wouldn't have had the slightest idea about rugby, let alone some guy called O'Driscoll who plays for Ireland in a tournament called the Six Nations.

Time to sign off. Catching a plane to London for a mystery assignation, probably the most important meeting of my career.

Wednesday 26 January, London

These are interesting times. Met yesterday evening with Clive Woodward at his home in Henley. Clive phoned me and suggested I come over for a 'chat', so I flew into Heathrow, and he picked me up at Arrivals and drove me to his lovely home, where we just talked and talked about the Lions. His wife Jayne rustled up some food, and it was all very relaxed. We talked about the Lions in general and about how I viewed the forthcoming New Zealand tour. Then we moved on to which British and Irish players I rated, what sort of game is needed to beat the All Blacks on their own turf. And then came the $64,000 question: how would I feel about captaining the Lions? It wasn't an offer as such, it was a hypothetical question – the crux of what amounted to the most important job interview of my life, albeit in the most laid-back and congenial of atmospheres.

It was definitely a moment I will remember for the rest of my life. The hairs went up on the back of my neck, just to hear Clive Woodward posing the question, to hear the exact words. My rugby life flashed in front of me, it really did. I had never realized before exactly how much it would mean to me to captain the Lions. I said 'Yes' with as much conviction and passion as I could muster. I then added that I was a big believer in the Martin Johnson approach of leading by example, but I didn't want to be a 'Johnno' clone. If invited, I would do it my way.

With that out of the way we went back to our general philosophies on the 2005 tour. We both agreed it should be fun – well, as much fun as it can be when you are trying to beat the All Blacks in their own backyard. I know a lot of the guys didn't greatly enjoy the 2001 trip to Australia, and a large group of players felt banished to the midweek side at a fairly early stage, where they didn't get the same back-up and preparation as the Test team. In fairness that wasn't Graham Henry's fault, the Lions simply didn't have enough back-up staff to do the job properly, and most of the resources went into the Saturday Test side. It is precisely to avoid this that Clive has enlarged the back-up team, basically setting up two different teams of coaches and medics.

But that's not the whole story. Clive believes that the

players ought to experience the country more, absorb the fantastic passion for rugby in New Zealand, enjoy the culture and a few decent nights out. Why not? It's a long tour and you have got to relax properly. If you were back home for that period of time you would certainly organize a few nights out and not necessarily on the beer. Just normal nights out. Why change when you tour abroad? We don't want any sort of siege mentality – that never works. Little Jack becomes a very dull boy if it is all work and no play.

There seems to be a misconception that Clive and I don't get on wonderfully well. From what I can judge it's all down to a fairly crass, although innocent enough, comment from yours truly before the Ireland–England match last year when I said something along the lines that an Ireland win would hopefully give the prawn sandwich brigade at Twickenham something to choke on.

It was a completely nothing comment, a rather lame attempt at humour on my part along the lines of something I had heard Roy Keane say about Manchester United's corporate supporters. I soon realized I might have stirred up a hornet's nest. Lawrence Dallaglio seemed to take it a little personally – he seemed more angry and pumped up than usual on the day of the match – and the comment has been dug out and used against me again recently, now that the issue of the Lions captaincy is being seriously discussed.

It seems out of all proportion, so I will have to be wary. Sarcastic humour might sound grand at the time on top table and get a laugh at press conferences but it rarely comes out like that in print in the cold light of day. And when you are trying to be funny, sometimes it just doesn't come out like you want it to. I must be much more careful. This is stuff that can be avoided.

Anyway, as far as I can judge it doesn't seem to be a problem with Clive. We got on fine. I love his enthusiasm and his big vision and the way he will leave no stone unturned to make sure the players are looked after. Flew home thinking that I had a decent shot at the captaincy, although Clive made it quite clear that no decisions would be made until after the Six Nations. Anything can happen in the next two months. Can't argue with that. Somehow I have to push Lions thoughts to one side now. Easier said than done, but Ireland must be the priority for the next two months.

Am writing these notes with my early-morning coffee. Got another big day ahead. It's coming at me from all directions at the moment.

Thursday 27 January, Clontarf

Yesterday was the official media launch of the Six Nations in London, with myself and coach Eddie O'Sullivan talking and posing for Ireland with our best Colgate ring-of-confidence smiles. Eddie turned up in some Buffalo Bill suede leather jacket, looking like he had just ridden in off the prairie. Very laid back. I was a boring git, regulation Ireland tracksuit and top as requested by the sponsors, although my sharp new haircut caused a few comments after the beachboy locks of last year. I am unrepentant about last year's look. Blonds have more fun, don't they?

The venue was amazing, a conference centre situated in a quaint Dickensian close, right under Westminster Abbey and the Houses of Parliament. Driving past, you would never guess that such a place existed. We did stacks of photo-shoots and TV interviews on the green before getting moved on by the choir boys of Westminster Abbey School, who put their coats down on the ground and enjoyed an old-fashioned game of pick-up football during their morning break.

Something wasn't quite right, and it was a while before I realized none of them were shouting or even talking. The game was played in complete silence. Apparently that's the deal, they have to protect their voices. Since I am struggling with a sore throat this morning, hoarse through waffling on in too many interviews, I know exactly where they are coming from.

Yesterday was a very tough day at the office in its own way, and I feel a bit battered mentally and vocally today. You are doing five or six set pieces for radio and TV – in between being dragged away for pics – and you try to treat every new interview as seriously as the previous one and give the same answers: otherwise you can look a prat and seem to be contradicting yourself when the articles appear. It's not easy, especially since occasionally there is that almost irresistible urge to cut loose and say something you know might not entirely concur with the party line. And sometimes a little mischievous thought worms its way into your mind: I wonder what would happen if I said something completely outrageous? You have to bury that one quickly, because you are on a hiding to nothing: the smallest things you say are picked up and amplified. I wouldn't necessarily say spun, because the words I am quoted as saying are pretty accurate, but they can be given undue prominence.

Half-way through the day, I ventured the opinion that world champions England had lost their aura. Considering they were now without Martin Johnson, Lawrence Dallaglio, the excellent Richard Hill, Neil Back and Jonny Wilkinson, to name but five World Cup heroes, I thought that was a fair enough comment and have heard a couple of noted former England captains say exactly the same in recent weeks. Like all sides, there always comes a time when the glory days end for a while and the rebuilding has to start in earnest. The words were innocent enough, but as soon as I saw everybody scribbling furiously – normally they just rely on their tape recorders – I realized I might be in trouble.

This morning, much as I had feared, some of the English papers chose to interpret my comments as Brian O'Driscoll having a dig at England and criticizing the current squad, which most certainly wasn't my intention. What to do? Become the most boring, say-nothing, diplomatic captain in history or call everything honestly and as I see it? I much prefer the latter and will just have to accept the consequences. In time and with luck my approach will earn a bit of respect in the long run.

Everybody seemed to be making us favourites. I actually think it is way too close to call and Ireland could just as easily finish third this season – but we certainly shouldn't hide from the 'favourites' tag. In fact, we have made a conscious decision in the squad to promote such a thought and embrace it early and get used to it. New Zealand are 'favourites' before just about every match they play and have to build that into their mentality and preparation.

We won the Triple Crown last year and have won four out of five championship matches for the past two seasons. We are playing France and England at home and people who understand the betting game, such as Ronan O'Gara, tell me that makes us the form-line favourites. OK, bring it on. Let's shoot for the stars. We have a settled, experienced, yet developing side. There is no reason why we shouldn't have a shout at the Championship, and maybe even the Grand Slam.

Thankfully I seemed to explain this much better than my misconstrued comments about England, and it didn't come over as Irish arrogance, merely justifiable confidence. I tried to emphasize that now was the time, this was the season for Ireland to aim high and achieve, not some other season somewhere in the future that may not ever present the same opportunity.

Back home now, having a meal with Mum and Dad and just chilling a little after a hectic couple of days. My shoulder is still wired up and unless it clears up overnight – and that is not unknown – it would be stupid to risk further damage playing for Leinster in the Gwent Dragons on Sunday night, much as I fancy a game after a couple of weeks on the sidelines.

Saturday 29 January, number 35

Had a run-out with Leinster at training yesterday. Shoulder felt considerably better but I went with my gut instinct and decided not to play against Gwent Dragons tomorrow. What I really need is a full week's training with Ireland ahead of the Italy game, and a little setback tomorrow would hinder that. I did an extra fitness session on the bike yesterday afternoon – really pushed it – to make amends and square the decision not to play in my mind. Then two big feature interviews with the main Irish papers, the *Irish Times* and the *Indo*.

The questions were excellent and thought-provoking. One of the journalists, who has known me all my rugby playing life, put it to me that I had grown and matured as a person and could now comfortably handle situations that would have fazed the bashful Brian O'Driscoll of five years ago. It was more of a statement than a question, but I couldn't have put it better myself. I nodded my agreement: it's exactly how I feel about myself at this moment and it was kinda nice that somebody was that interested to notice my development as a person.

Sunday 30 January, City West

Here we go. Back into camp to prepare for our opener against Italy. Arrived this evening – all the Leinster boys are coming in after a brilliant 55–3 win over the Dragons, our best performance in a good while. Seems like I wasn't missed that much, in fact not at all! Gordon D'Arcy in great form, really beginning to fly after his injury problems. Glad for him, he has had a rough ride since last summer when he went lame in South Africa and is a key man for us if he can reproduce the form of last season. Intend getting an earlyish night, big week ahead, want to get some sleep in the bank. Listening to Christy Moore on the sound system. Wanted something mellow and thought-provoking going around my head. It's a long build-up to internationals these days and I like to keep things very low-key and relaxed early in the week – the madness and excitement will kick in soon enough.

Tuesday 1 February, City West

I'm a rugby player, get me out of here! It's the hanging around that gets you down. I seem to have been talking and thinking about this year's Six Nations for ever, and a ball hasn't been kicked in anger yet. I've played it over in my head at least three times. I've said everything I want to say about ten times. All we want to do is get out there and play.

Today we announced our side to play Italy, and it seemed to meet with general approval. Potentially this is as incisive and dangerous an Ireland back division as we have ever fielded, certainly in my time. Gordon D'Arcy, who has been ripping it in training and making everybody look like cart-horses, is alongside me in the centre; Shaggy, another in excellent form, goes out to the wing; and Geordan Murphy drops back to full-back at the expense of Girvan Dempsey. I am bloody excited at the prospect of this back division clicking.

Girvan is a seriously underrated player, both for Ireland and Leinster, but there can be no sentiment in sport. Everybody gets dropped or loses form at some stage and Geordan Murphy is a player we have to get the best out of if we are to give the Championship a real rattle.

I am biased because Geordie is a great mate, but I sincerely believe he is the most talented and skilful rugby player I have ever played with or against. He does incredible things on the training field and lifts the whole atmosphere, the rest of us trying to match his trickery.

His broken leg on the eve of the 2003 World Cup was a massive blow, no matter how hard we tried to play it down. Geordie was our secret weapon – the rugby world at large hadn't really clocked him – and he was in the form of his life. He would have been a sensation down in Australia. Since then, if I am honest, he hasn't quite recaptured that magic at international level; it needs something to happen to reignite his confidence on the big stage. The injury is fine – he is fit and he is still firing on all cylinders at training – but now comes the acid test.

There has been a lot of talk about Darce perhaps encountering a second-season syndrome after his stellar Six Nations last season, when he was voted player of the tournament. I don't buy into that at all. Name the last quality player who endured a second-season syndrome? A quality player is a quality player. End of story. He will be grand, believe me.

Up front it's all the usual suspects with one change, Denis Leamy getting the nod over Johnny O'Connor at openside flanker. A tight call. Denis is a very strong young guy and a powerful ball-carrier, and we are expecting a huge physical challenge from the Italians, but Johnny is a great link man and good on the floor to ensure quick possession. With our first-choice back division finally on the pitch we want to play to our strengths, and quick possession is a must. Yes, a very tight call.

Six Nations

Friday 4 February, St Regis Grand Hotel, Rome

Air temperature: 12 degrees. Forecast: a stormy seven weeks in store. Atmosphere: tense. Feeling edgy – which is normally a good sign – except this is Friday afternoon and a bit early for the butterflies to start fluttering before a Sunday match. The first game of a Six Nations tournament is always tricky, no matter who you are playing, and I suppose the memory of our last Ireland performance – that shocker against Argentina – is still fresh.

Italy are no mugs and concern me a little. They seem to produce their best Championship performances first up, maybe before injuries and their lack of strength in depth kick in. They have beaten Scotland and Wales in opening games before, and we were flattered by the scoreline two years ago at the Stadio Flaminio.

They are far more structured and organized under John Kirwan. They have learned from other sides, bringing in various little plays. They are fast becoming a smart team, harder and harder to bring down. The days of Italy being the whipping boys are long behind us.

Monday 7 February (i), St Regis Grand Hotel

Nearly 1 a.m. Monday at our hotel in the Via Vittorio Emmanuel. Sitting here in the team room icing my bloody hamstring and feeling sorry for myself. Gordon D'Arcy is here doing the same – his hamstring went after just twenty minutes – and Donncha O'Callaghan is escaping the post-match formalities as he nurses a knock on his hand. Mike Ford, our defensive coach, and Mervyn Murphy, our video analyst, and a couple of the wives and girlfriends are here as well, looking after us. Trying not to get too depressed, but a long haul back to fitness awaits, starting now, if I am to feature much more in the Six Nations. Time for a pot of tea and a few sandwiches. I'm not throwing the towel in just yet.

What was I doing, anyway, scrambling around with their pack in the last minute? I need my head examined. The match was well won. It just didn't matter whether they got a consolation try or not. I should have been boxing clever. We have a big match against Scotland at Murrayfield in six days' time. And now this. Why me?

Need another sandwich, famished. I am being too harsh on myself. Of course it mattered. It's a physical game and I am a physical player who gets stuck in from start to finish. It's the only way I know how. You can't just turn it on and off. And you can get injured any time. It is illogical to beat myself up. The exact same injury could have happened in the first half, when the scores were really tight, and I wouldn't be asking these questions.

What happened? I was rushing back in defence as the Italian forwards started to rumble dangerously near our line, and I was taking a lot of weight through my left leg as I tried to poach the ball. Suddenly the maul surged forward, again, my leg taking the strain, and collapsed on me. I knew straight away that I had to get off the pitch, there was no point in trying to hobble and play the hero.

I was pretty worried because I have torn my hamstring five or six times. I could write a book on the various grades of hamstring tears, prognosis, rehab programme and repair time. It's probably that Irish thing of long back, short legs and lots of straining muscles and tendons that does for me. Our physio Brian Green put me straight on to his mobile physio's couch and started prodding around very gently. It was pretty sore, but I have known worse.

Often he has found a hole − literally − in the hamstring, and when he locates that I normally hit the ceiling. On other occasions I have felt like I have been shot or stabbed in the leg − nasty piercing pain. This one was more of a pop. I knew it wasn't great but I knew it wasn't as bad as some others.

Got changed and went back on the bus to the hotel − rest of the boys went off to do a pool session, aware that Scotland was looming and that every minute of preparation and rehab time is precious. The more energetic were planning a small run ashore, nothing drastic, just a way of killing time really. When you have played a full-on international there is no way you can even think about getting to sleep until the early hours, the adrenalin is pumping so hard. You are better off enjoying a bit of down-time with friends and family than pacing around your room staring at the four walls.

Monday 7 February (ii), St Regis Grand Hotel

Just gone noon. Still here in the team room, it feels as if I never moved. Finally turned in about 2.30 a.m., my leg red and burning from the ice. Our flight home to Dublin is delayed for a couple of hours, but at least the airline phoned ahead, which means we can spend the time in the comfort of our hotel, and myself and Darce can continue the endless icing and compressing routine which you need during the first thirty-six hours of a bad hammie.

Clive Woodward has been on, inquiring after my health, and I told him honestly that we weren't sure yet, but my gut feeling was that it wasn't completely ripped and it could be weeks rather than months. Please, God, let that be true.

Meanwhile, what about the game? I've had a chat with a few of the lads now and seen the video. We were pretty poor, but good enough and experienced enough to take our opportunities and grind out a win. We must improve drastically on that for the coming matches.

We were very dodgy in the first twenty minutes and struggled in a big way. We didn't own the ball, we didn't see the ball. And when we did, ROG and the other kickers had great trouble finding touch. Their big forwards rumbled it up just as we knew they would, but we just didn't get out of the blocks, and I am pretty disappointed about that. We guessed they were going to have a purple patch, but we didn't think it would be for twenty minutes, and the first twenty minutes at that! Just give me the ball in my hands, I was screaming to myself. I knew we could do some serious damage, one-on-one, against the Italian backs.

Ireland have become prone to slow starts, although we flew out of the blocks against Wales last season. It's a worry. Can't put my finger on any one thing that is going wrong. We go out with every good intention, but it's definitely something to look at.

All it takes is seemingly one innocuous incident to put you

on the back foot, the opposition gain a little bit of momentum and everything snowballs. If you give them anything, they quickly raise their game to your level. That is especially important when you are underdogs. 'Smaller' sides try to gain a foothold early with a big hit or a big play. Ireland should know, because for many years that has been our approach.

Midway through the first half I managed to create a try for Geordie, which eased the pressure a bit. I had just had an accidental clash of heads with Darce and was feeling a little bit woozy. It was just going to be a set-up with Denis Leamy. Darce, probably thinking I still wasn't quite at the races, suggested I step in at twelve. I said, 'Grand, whatever, no problems,' and we swapped positions. As I went across I saw there might be a bit of space, and then the Red Sea opened up and I hit the turbo on a really nice outside arc, the sort you see in coaching videos and diagrams. It wasn't quite training-ground stuff, because it was actually a variation on the planned move, but you have to react to what you see in front of you. I felt great. We had been under the cosh and I wanted to show the boys how I thought we could make this game easier on ourselves.

We got a couple of tries through Peter Stringer and Denis Hickie in the second half, but still the fluency wouldn't come and we did nothing more than manufacture a win on an afternoon when we underperformed – but sometimes you have to do that when you get to a certain level. If you want to be considered one of the best teams in the world you can't have slip-ups against teams you would expect to beat. You just can't. How many times do Australia and New Zealand slip up against lesser teams – and when I say lesser I also mean the likes of ourselves, Wales and Scotland? How many times do New Zealand and Australia ever lose in those circumstances?

Close calls, yes. Defeats? Hardly ever. We did the Aussies at Lansdowne Road two years ago and that's it.

When the Aussies or the Blacks play poorly they still win by two or three points. No team can fire on all cylinders all the time, but when you are having a middling day you have to make sure you do enough to win the game. After yesterday's victory it is a case of filing it in the memory bank and seeing where we need to improve. And let's look on the bright side. I've just seen the Six Nations table on BBC online: despite a dodgy performance, Ireland are top!

Monday 7 February (iii), City West

Nearly 10.30 p.m. and finally back at Mission Control for more treatment on the hamstring, followed by a quick pool session before 'retiring hurt' to my bedroom. What a day! We eventually got to the airport and I hobbled on to the plane, where the IRFU had somehow managed to reserve two rows of three seats apiece for myself and Darce so we could stretch out. Although we need to spend two or three days on crutches, we discarded them walking through Dublin airport in case the photographers were around. No point in letting the Scots know that the two of us were completely banjaxed!

From the airport it was straight into a waiting taxi and a battle through the evening rush-hour out to the Dublin suburb of Finglas, where Dr Steve Eustace was waiting patiently to oversee our MRI scans and pronounce on the injuries. These scans, which involve disappearing into a space-age tunnel, are definitely an acquired taste. They can be extremely claustrophobic and panic-inducing, especially for the big guys from the pack.

Keith Wood used to go through a thousand agonies when he had his neck and shoulders scanned after various injuries and operations, a process that can take a full hour. Keith used to ask the nurse to tickle his feet for the duration to provide some sort of mental and physical distraction. Well, that's his excuse! Luckily, because it was just my hamstring, I could go in feet first and the scan was only twenty-five minutes long. Earphones on, eyeshades on, and wake me up when you are finished, please, sir.

Steve then went into action. I've known him ever since I first broke into the Ireland side. He always drops everything to help out and is virtually on first-name terms with my hamstrings and adductors. We have our own jargon for them. He immediately put my mind at rest and said he had seen worse. He was quite positive, really, and estimated between two and four weeks' recovery time, tending towards the latter. The diagnosis on Darce was similar, if anything slightly more optimistic.

So definitely no Scotland and a major fight on our hands to get fit for England. Somehow I felt a bit better – it wasn't all doom and gloom – and immediately spoke to Eddie. The Scots had looked very good against France in Paris on Sunday – with a bit of luck they could have won – and they will be taking a lot of momentum into the game at Murrayfield. We have to try everything to throw them off track. They might have suspected that myself and Darce were in serious trouble, but the beauty is they have no way of knowing for sure. Let's keep it that way. Why not leave them guessing as long as possible? This is professional sport. Let's be professional. Best to name the two of us and leave it late in the week before we withdraw. We might not fool them for one second. but it would be nice to see them scratching their heads a little. They might be facing an Ireland side with myself and Darce in the centre, but then again it might be Shane Horgan and Kevin Maggs if we drop out. Then again we might ask the versatile Geordan to move into the centre with Shaggy and bring in a new full-back, or perhaps bring Girvan back at full-back and introduce young Tommy Bowe on the wing. If they have to work on two or even three separate lots of analysis and yet, at the same time, think in their minds that some of this is a waste of time, that's grand. It's got to be an irritant and distraction. We are not here to make life easy for them. Let's do what Scotland least want us to do.

Thursday 10 February, City West

Tough grinding week, working around the clock with the medics on my hamstring. Lots of exercises in the pool and physio treatment. The papers still say myself and Darce are in the team and hopefully the Scots have taken that on board. Neither of us will be travelling to Edinburgh today – we can't afford the time away from treatment – so our little ruse will be blown. Actually I think my withdrawal is going to be announced officially this afternoon and Gordon apparently is going to have a 'fitness test' tomorrow morning. I can tell you exactly what the result will be!

The truth is we are off on a little trip together. It has been decided that the two of us are going to fly to the infamous Cryotherapy Chambers in Spala in central Poland on Sunday for five days' intensive treatment to try to make sure that we are fit for the England game. We have been there before with Ireland for intensive training camps – it was Warren Gatland who started the trend when he was Ireland coach. We would go in the middle of the summer, when midges and mosquitoes added to the pain. Spartan doesn't even begin to describe it. But it fits the bill exactly now: an all-mod-cons fitness centre with the added attraction that its super-cooled ice chambers – where they can set the temperature to minus 120 degrees – enable you to triple your workload on any given day. The theory, and I can confirm it works in practice, is that the extreme cold boosts your circulation and flushes out the lactic acid and other toxins that exercise releases into the system. It should accelerate our recovery by perhaps two weeks. Worth a go, without a doubt. If we can squeeze past Scotland on Saturday, our season could hinge on the England match. If we can be three out of three after that game we really will be in business.

Paul O'Connell will captain against Scotland in my absence, as he did against France last year. Paul got very nervous on that occasion about his post-match speech, a situation enlivened somewhat when he discovered that his opposite number, Fabien Pelous – a veteran of countless captain's speeches – had nicked his notes. Hopefully Scotland's Gordon Bulloch doesn't share Fabien's sense of humour.

Saturday 12 February, Great Southern Hotel, Dublin airport

Air temperature: 6 degrees. Forecast: it's going to get much colder! Atmosphere: apprehensive. It's just gone 10 p.m. and I've checked into the Great Southern for our crack-of-dawn flight to Poland tomorrow. It's the only way to get any sleep. Waiting for my alarm clock to go off back home and relying on the taxi to arrive on time is a recipe for disaster. I wouldn't settle at all. Anyway, I've enjoyed a couple of relaxing days back home after checking out of City West. I wanted to watch the Scotland game on my own, although in the end my sister Jules called in for a cuppa, which was fine. Hate watching matches I should be involved in — I don't know a player who does — but I made myself sit down and tried to make a few mental notes. This is a really intense time of the season and all sorts of small things you see might help when you come to the debrief and preparing for England.

It's strange. You're sitting there knowing, up to a point, what is going to happen, but I had missed out on the training all week and didn't know the fine detail of the moves we had planned. I could see what we were doing with certain set-ups, but not always. I find it very uncomfortable watching when you have no power over anything. It must be complete hell being a parent watching your kids from the touchline every weekend. An interesting little insight into why my dad gets so wound up!

We started like drains again. What is it about us in the first twenty minutes? We really have got to get this sorted out because it will cost us dear against class sides. We got away lightly against Italy because they didn't kick their goals and Scotland could have had at least one more try after scoring a very decent effort early on through Hugo Southwell. That said, it was no coincidence that Scotland did score just the once, because our defence and tackling were superb. We just need to get on the front foot earlier in our games.

That's the bad news. The good news is that we stayed calm, as I knew we would, and that Paul O'Connell and the pack rolled up their sleeves and crucified the Scots for the next hour with a magnificent display of 'old style Munster' rugby, as one scribe described it. I know what he meant, we just squeezed the life out of the Scots pack, allowing Peter Stringer and ROG to dictate the game at half-back. ROG was back to his best, kicking the ball sweetly after his problems in Rome. We never looked back and scored five good tries to run out convincing 40–13 winners. It could have been even more, with Shaggy unluckily spilling the ball over the line, but we must not be greedy. It was an excellent away win and makes me more determined than ever to get back for England.

So, just wishing the hours away here, listening to a few sounds and texting the boys in Edinburgh. Bit worrying how both Leinster and Ireland seem to have produced belting performances without me in recent weeks!

Sunday 13 February, en route to Spala, Poland

Luckily there is a direct flight from Dublin to Warsaw these days – when we have travelled to Poland before it's been via a three-hour stopover in Copenhagen. This is much better. Just waking up at 37,000 feet after operating on autopilot for our 6 a.m. departure time.

Getting out of Dublin was all a bit cloak and dagger, like something from a Michael Caine film. Good fun, though. The IRFU had booked us under different names to try to shake off press and public interest. I was Brendan O'Donovan and Darce was Graham Delaney. I quite liked my new identity, it had a nice theatrical ring to it, I thought, a young actor from the Abbey Theatre perhaps, trekking out to Warsaw in the middle of winter to study mime. Or perhaps a trad musician from the West on the way to a couple of gigs in

Warsaw's Irish pubs. Wonder if Brendan is married or has a gorgeous girlfriend or what the story is with him? Would like to know more.

Darce wasn't so impressed with Graham Delaney – he sounded a bit of a strait-laced Irish EU agricultural officer visiting his Polish counterpart to discuss pig-feed quotas or dairy-herd yields. No doubt they would end up drinking Guinness together in one of Warsaw's Irish pubs. In fact they would probably end up singing along to Brendan O'Donovan.

Embarrassing moment when I checked in. Couldn't remember if I was meant to maintain the pretence about the names or if the ground crew were in on the subterfuge. Net result was, when I was asked my name, I just froze as if it was the most difficult question in the world. I grinned inanely, something at which I am rather good, allegedly. Say something, guys! The ground crew didn't relent, or just thought I was the village idiot. Clearly I would never make it as a secret agent.

In fact the whole early morning was totally off the wall and not a drop taken for weeks and weeks. Waiting in the departure lounge before boarding, a middle-aged lady in sensible tweeds asked me if I was the young actor in the O_2 advert on television. Didn't really know if this was a compliment or an insult. I took it as the former. Either that or there is an actor out there that Leinster or Eddie O'Sullivan ought to take a serious look at. Both said lady and myself were half asleep, so it was a slightly surreal conversation, and it was with some relief that I stumbled to my seat, switched on the sounds and drifted off. Sleep deprivation can definitely mess with your head, and I made a small promise to myself to avoid ridiculously early flights for the rest of my life.

Monday 14 February, Spala

Arrived safely yesterday. About two hours' drive from Warsaw. Bloody cold, but nothing compared with what they had here last week, apparently, when it dropped to minus 20. It's just about freezing today, but there is a biting wind and the dirty, stained snow is piled high by the sides of the road. Everything is like an old black-and-white film. There's no colour or brightness. St Barth's it ain't, but then again we are not here on holiday, we are here to work 24/7 at getting our knackered hamstrings in shape.

Darce has just reminded me it's Valentine's Day. Not a card to be seen, although given my recent record on the romance front this is probably the best place for me at present. I've just glanced at our schedule for the day. Not exactly champagne and roses. At least there are some gorgeous female athletes to admire as we run around, doing our stuff. Some of them are in incredible physical condition, they completely put us to shame. Didn't know women had six-packs, and they must score zero on the dreaded pinch test. Gordon and I will be spending a lot of time sucking our stomachs in and trying to look the part.

Tuesday 15 February, Spala

Here, for the record, is how I spent Valentine's Day 2005 with my very special friend, Gordon D'Arcy. Bit lacking on the romance front. 'Roses are red, violets are blue, your hamstring is knackered, it's cryo for you!'

8.45 Reveille. Rise and shine except it's still dark outside. Is that a wolf howling in the woods?

9.00 Breakfast: cereal, bread, frankfurter, hot chocolate. My body is a temple.

9.30 First cryotherapy session of the day. We have ways of making you talk, Mr O'Donovan

9.45 Pool (aqua-jogging, running, lengths)

10.30 Track. Acceleration drills, speed work, bio-mechanics

11.00 Coffee break. Actually forty-five minutes, crashed out on my bed

11.45 Cryotherapy session. Why am I here, Darce? Remind me again?

12.20 Fitness work on the static bikes

13.25 Lunch (optional): cereal, bread, frankfurter, beetroot, hot chocolate

13.45 Break/sleep

15.30 Weights or skills or both

17.00 Cryotherapy session. There is no escape, Mr O'Donovan. That is your name, isn't it?

17.45 Massage. Go to reception to see if any Red Cross parcels have arrived

18.15 Physio treatment

19.15 Dinner! Walk to the restaurant. Choice of bread, frankfurter, battered steak, beetroot, hot chocolate

21.30 Bed. Try watching a DVD with Darce, but we fall asleep making plans to escape.

Thursday 17 February, Spala

Air temperature: minus 127 degrees! Forecast: it can only get warmer. Atmosphere: arctic. Just finished my final cryo session. Nearly done here and I won't shed any tears when we drive back to Warsaw tomorrow. But I have to say the trip has been thoroughly worthwhile: the transformation has been phenomenal. I was doing some very light jogging before I left; now I'm virtually flat out. We've worked through the pain barrier a bit and I feel as if I am back on course.

The cryo treatment isn't a wonder cure in itself, but it definitely helps the blood circulation, which in turn helps a bit with repairing damaged muscles. It's exactly what it says on the tin: it means you can triple your workload without over-stressing damaged muscles and joints.

We were worked like horses in the pool with the bungee straps or cords. Brian Green would be running alongside and by the last ten metres of the pool we would really be going flat out. Then there was all the stuff we did in the shallow end – hips, crossovers, flipper stuff with boards and basically getting the length back into our strides.

There were three cryo sessions a day. The challenge is to stay in as long as you are able and no longer than is safe. GD could last about five or six minutes, I sometimes made it to eight – according to Darce on account of my excess body fat. Cheeky bugger. The chambers are staffed by medics at all times, monitoring your blood pressure by the second, because in such cold you can become disorientated or pass out.

When you come out – at the risk of stating the bloody obvious – you feel freezing cold and numb, so it's a great time to hop on to the exercise bikes and do some extra fitness work, working like maniacs to warm up.

We had everything we wanted on site and we had nothing else to do. Cryo, massage, physio, gym, track, weights room, pool, the works. There was none of the hassle you might get in Dublin of travelling around the city, trying to find a physio, making an appointment here, booking in a scan there, waiting for a consultant. There was absolutely nothing to do but concentrate on getting fit.

To kill time every evening, Darce, Brian and I would walk to a so-called restaurant half a mile up the road with Ziggy, our translator. Whatever Ziggy ordered always looked the same, was covered in egg batter and tasted dire. On the way back it would be pitch dark with sheet ice everywhere and strange noises coming from the nearby woodlands. More than once it occurred to me that slipping on the ice and breaking a leg, or being savaged by a pack of Polish wolves, would be a pretty strange way to bale out of the Six Nations.

To be frank, Spala is a miserable, miserable place – especially at this time of year – and the lads were laughing their heads off when they heard we had been banished there. It has worked for me, though, and I am grateful. Completely confident of taking a full part in training with Ireland next week and lining up against England.

Haven't had much contact from home – hardly surprising considering I changed my mobile number just before we left after a bout of nuisance calls. They can be pretty frustrating, but I've developed a new approach to dealing with them. Every number I want or need is saved to the phone. If a private number comes up I just answer my phone and put it back in my pocket so I'm wasting the caller's credit and annoying them. I just don't entertain them for a second, don't get into any conversations, don't even tell them to piss off. I got one call on the morning of the England Grand Slam match in 2003 from some kids and completely lost it. I ranted away, telling them how insensitive they were, and it hit home a bit. They realized they had overstepped the mark. I have become far more thick-skinned since then.

Friday 18 February, number 35

Arrived back in one piece, but only just. After a couple of hours' sightseeing to kill time before our flight, we were on our way to Warsaw airport when our taxi driver, who to be frank was pushing it too hard, had to take evasive action as one of those large twin-carriaged buses slid slightly out of control on a roundabout. We smacked into the side of the bus with a frightening thud. Luckily no serious damage was done to either the driver or his Irish passengers, but the car looked a mess. Strange trip. Successful, but I was very glad to get home. Starving – what with working around the clock and eating frugally, I've lost half a stone. Must try to not pig out when I am reintroduced to proper food tonight.

Saturday 19 February, number 35

Ignore my last. Pigged out and now feeling very full. First proper meal for nearly a week. Read a few papers to catch up on the gossip and the mobile is red hot from those in the squad inquiring politely after my health. I tell them, politely, that Spala was gorgeous and I am planning a holiday there in August.

Tuesday 22 February, City West

Apparently Paul O'Connell is to captain the Lions in New Zealand. *The Times* of London has the story, so it must be official. Lots of banter at breakfast this morning with POC getting plenty of stick and elaborate congratulations from the lads and requests that he put in a good word next time he is talking to Sir Clive. The two of us enjoyed a good laugh about it. Neither of us has a clue what is really going on or where the story came from.

He would be a good selection. POC is developing into a fantastic second row and he is very bright and clever. He is not just an old-style fire-and-brimstone Munster forward, he thinks on the hoof and knows exactly what he is doing. He trains like a maniac, absolutely full-on, and I always take good care to keep out of his way when possible in the full-contact stuff. There's no doubt he did a good job captaining Ireland in my absence at Murrayfield the other week, and we reckon that's where the bandwagon really started about him cap-taining the Lions. A lot of people are drawing the comparison between him and Martin Johnson, both as players and characters.

No surprises in the team today. I am good to go, so return at centre, but Darce has not made it, not for the want of trying on his part. So I am reunited with Shane Horgan at centre, with Girvan on the wing. We are expecting, and preparing, to meet the 'real' England on Sunday. Got a feeling they will finally hit their stride, so we had better be good.

Thursday 24 February, City West

Sloped out this evening with Geordan Murphy to watch, and support, his girlfriend Lucie Silvas, who was singing at a big pop awards night in Dublin. We didn't want any of the VIP treatment that the organizers suggested – there are those who believe you should be tucked up in bed at 10 p.m. with a hot chocolate four days before an international – we just wanted to disappear in the crowd and enjoy a relaxing night. Which we did. Lucie is superb, very talented. Not just a singer but a real musician who writes most of her own stuff. Very creative, bit like Geordan himself. Just got back now, not long after ten. No harm done and feeling very relaxed.

Monday 28 February, number 35

Very sore this morning. Moving around the kitchen like an old man of ninety. Got some rehab and a pool session later. Should help.

Just cannot believe the fuss England and their press are making after their 19–13 defeat against us yesterday. Apparently they were 'robbed blind' thanks to 'appalling' refereeing by Jonathan Kaplan. Excuse me, were they watching the same game?

When you are involved with a fair bit of Test rugby, either as a player or coach, you have to get used to the rub of the green. Decisions go against you but, more often than you probably care to admit, little fifty–fifty calls go in your favour as well. Funny how you never seem to remember those. I just can't believe England are whingeing about this match, particularly head coach Andy Robinson. Their reaction is way out of proportion.

Kaplan did OK. As far as I can see, he made one blatantly bad call – and if I got through a match with only one bad unforced error I would consider it a good afternoon's work. In the first half he and his linesman missed Danny Grewcock clearly blocking ROG on the fringe of a ruck. This allowed Martin Corry to pick up and waltz over for an important first-half score which rocked us back a bit. I saw exactly what happened but knew there was no point in arguing. Kaplan had made the call and we had to get on with the game.

As for the two decisions that went against England, the Josh Lewsey 'try' that never was really never was. He was held up over the line, failed to get the touchdown and was then pushed back. Scrum Ireland. Referee right on the spot. Correct decision. No need to go to the video ref, and in fact, as the action ended back up in the field of play, I believe that the laws actually state that the video ref should not be used in such circumstances.

Mark Cueto's 'try' from Charlie Hodgson's crossfield kick was a close call, no doubt about it. My gut instinct was that he was a yard in front, but it was brilliantly executed, hours on the Sale training ground no doubt, and it certainly wasn't offside by design.

If the call had gone against us there would have been no whingeing. As it was, Mr Kaplan was again in an excellent position and made his judgement. He thought Cueto was just in front. And even if the try had been allowed, who is to say England would have emerged as winners? It was a nip-and-tuck game. Although England were playing well, I never doubted we would always find the points to finish ahead when the final whistle came.

When we heard of Andy Robinson's post-match outburst at the England press conference it was obvious England were trying to deflect attention from a third straight defeat, create a diversion if you like. Robbo seems to be getting into a bit of hot water today, with talk of him being charged with 'bringing the game into disrepute'.

It is all bloody unsatisfactory, really, though it doesn't take the gloss off one of our best-ever wins. England produced their most impressive rugby for a year. This was a much harder-earned win than our victory at Twickenham twelve months ago, when England just didn't turn up.

The match went exactly as I thought it would, I never anticipated winning by more than one score, although there was a moment in the second half when we should have made it 22–13 and maybe we could have put some space between ourselves and England.

It started with what people thought was a drama. In fact it wasn't as bad as it looked. I know from experience that you can get freezing cold with the prolonged preliminaries at Lansdowne Road – what with the presentations to our President, Mary MacAleese, the away-team anthem and then Ireland's two anthems. I was determined to keep my hamstring warm. We had been getting loads of heat into it all week and it would have been a shame for it to all go wrong in the fifteen minutes or so of hanging around, so I had arranged for our masseur Willie Bennett to nip out and keep working on it. There was nothing wrong, it wasn't pulling or anything, I just wanted to try to prevent that happening. I was straight into action from the off, making a full-pelt run down the touchline, and was very gratified that all seemed well.

Our try was grand, good work from Denis Hickie, lovely

little dummy and inside step by Geordie and a helping hand by Charlie Hodgson, trying to intercept, that slowed the pass down nicely as it came my way. I was actually screaming at Geordan to chip ahead because there was no full-back at home and the try line was beckoning, but it worked out fine. I had stepped out into touch a couple of times in getting into position but had just enough room to squeeze through – there must have been at least half an inch to spare.

Given the state of the match it was important that I get around under the posts as far as possible, which is what I did, although I admit I didn't finish off in the most elegant style. Big Joe Worsley was tracking back to stop me from getting under the posts. I didn't want to tangle with him and pick up an unnecessary injury, that would have been too stupid for words, so I decided to slide in, keeping the ball off the ground for as long as possible to gain a few extra yards. A disappointing 5.1 for style but a gorgeous seven points on the scoreboard, which was the only thing that mattered.

We defended brilliantly late in the second half when England threw the kitchen sink at us. Clever, scientific defence as well as hard physical tackling and spoiling. We pressed hard but always kept six inches back from the offside line. Very proud about the way we protected our lead. One of those occasions when the hours of defensive routines with coach Mike Ford – and, God, can they ever be boring – paid off handsomely.

After the game it was pleasing to see that we reacted as if it was just another win against another big side. We didn't go mad or potty because it was England. I was very encouraged by that. You have to try to temper the highs and lows a bit. The 'great' wins are not normally quite as great as you think and the bad defeats are rarely quite as bad either.

With two weeks before the France game I fancied a late night and hitting a club with some of the England boys, but these Sunday matches are pretty hopeless socially. The mood is never the same, fans are heading for home and players have to put on their club hats and start thinking of the week ahead. We ground to a halt much earlier than normal. Nowhere seemed to be open late. It is often the second night after a good win when you can savour it best with your friends and colleagues.

Tuesday 1 March, number 35

The voice of reason has emerged. The England captain Martin Corry, who had a fantastic match, has admitted that England 'stuffed up' and that Mr Kaplan cannot be blamed in any way. Honest words from a very tough and honest player.

Still unbelievably stiff and sore after Sunday, I can't remember ever taking so long to get a game out of my system. Half of the problem is that I picked up a dead leg, courtesy of a big tackle from Jamie Noon, and really you need a bit of a run around, if not the day after then the next day, to work off a lot of the soreness. It's the old Tour de France thing: the cyclists have to go for a ride on their day off, otherwise they will seize up completely. The other factor is that I have felt under a huge amount of pressure the last fortnight – the first week just working my butt off in Poland and striving to get fit and the second week obviously building up for a huge match against England. I'm suffering a bit of a reaction but need to shake it off quickly.

Off to London tomorrow night for the North v South tsunami benefit game at Twickenham. No chance of me playing, alas, not with my dead leg, but as the nominated captain I'm keen to try to help generate some more publicity, and money, by doing some of the press stuff and meeting a few sponsors. Clive Woodward, coach of the North side, has organized a team dinner, so it will be good to meet some of the guys in pretty relaxed circumstances. There is also an Adidas advert to shoot for the Lions, which could be fun. Bit superstitious about doing this particular one, what with the Lions squad nowhere near picked yet, but apparently they have to be filmed well in advance. Having said that, I'm growing to enjoy these occasions more and more. You are becoming a media tart, Drico!

Sunday 6 March, City West

Was still a little worried about my leg so headed home from London on Friday afternoon for more treatment and rest and a couple of nights' sleep in my own bed. You cannot believe how luxurious and relaxing that is after being on the road or confined to barracks, albeit four-star barracks, at City West. Pure bliss, and I was feeling happy with life when I checked back in earlier tonight. The leg is definitely easing and I feel confident of getting through a full week's training, which will be all-important going into a huge match against the French.

Tuesday 8 March, City West

The Grand Slam hype has started in earnest. Bit strange, because we were very open before the tournament started and said we were gunning for it, but nobody seemed to believe us then! And of course, having now discovered that their team has a decent chance, the Irish public and media are going a little overboard, dismissing the French game as if it's just a small hurdle to get over before it's onwards and upwards to Cardiff for the mother of all games, because nobody doubts that Wales will inflict some serious damage on Scotland at Murrayfield.

Feel a little uneasy. Wales escaped with a fantastic win in Paris, but France should have been twenty-five points ahead at half-time and out of sight after playing the best out-and-out attacking rugby the Championship has seen for a few years. Wales had two try-scoring chances after the break, took them both brilliantly and then defended like heroes to claim a fabulous win, but that, in my mind, doesn't disguise the fact that France were the better side on the day and are possibly emerging as the best team in the Championship,

Bad news for Darce. He played on Sunday for Leinster and did OK, but the hamstring still isn't right. He says it's 95 per cent healed, but when he really wants to hit the gas the power just isn't there and the muscle feels very vulnerable. Know exactly how he feels. If there is going to be a problem it is always during that last phase of the recovery when it flares up. Makes me feel very lucky to sneak through on the blind side, so to speak. We are missing Shaggy with a broken hand, and Kevin Maggs again, so that's fine, but very conscious that we need all our big guns firing to get over the final two hurdles. Gordon is a world-class centre capable of doing something special to turn a game.

Thursday 10 March, City West

Not in good form this evening. Our training session today was pretty shambolic. Eddie wasn't happy at all – and rightly so – and he said a few choice words, so we took it on ourselves to organize an extra team meeting tonight to try to iron a few things out.

Nothing unusual in having a couple of dodgy sessions in the course of a seven-week tournament or a long tour – it's just the equivalent of the occasional bad day at the office that everybody in every walk of life experiences. I remember reading once that when Wales won their last Grand Slam in 1978, back in the amateur days, they were such a shambles on the previous Sunday that the coach John Dawes looked on for just five minutes before ordering them all to put their feet up or spend an afternoon on the golf course. Some days, for whatever reason, the concentration and intensity just aren't there. It is good coaching to recognize that, rein back and spend the rest of the day playing snooker or something.

What is unnerving today is that we are so close to the game. If you have a bad session early in the week you invariably rectify it with a full-on, eyeballs-out effort the next day which wipes the slate clean. We haven't got that opportunity now, we have just our normal, light Friday run-out with the kickers doing another half hour at Lansdowne Road.

Clive Woodward has been with us all this week. True to his word he stayed totally in the background, just observing. There was a fair bit of banter going around among the lads, though. Italy and France got murdered when he spent a week observing in the autumn and Wales also lost against New

Zealand, although to be fair they played superbly. Is he a jinx? We will find out on Saturday.

Paul O'Connell – a candidate along with me for the Lions captaincy if you believe what you read in the press – took a fair ribbing last night when I, the school swot and a creep of the first order, made three reasonably coherent points in a team meeting in front of Sir Clive. POC, in contrast, chose to keep his own counsel! He probably just thought I was talking my usual crap. Perhaps he was the wise one. Silence can be golden.

Saturday 12 March, Berkeley Court Hotel, Dublin

Sitting here in my hotel room with the intention of making a few notes about our defeat against France before going downstairs to the bar and lobby to face the world again with a smiley face. Just can't find the words. More disappointed than I can ever remember, and we have suffered much heavier losses than this. Can't see how Ireland will ever make the breakthrough. This was our chance. These opportunities come around once in a generation for small sides like us. Utterly pissed off. Feel completely crushed and empty. We could have won, but let's be honest: we froze. How are we ever going to get ourselves up for Wales now? I'm the captain, it's up to me to do something. Will try to write again tomorrow. Bollocks to everything.

Monday 14 March, City West

Air temperature: 8 degrees. Forecast: very tough week ahead. Atmosphere: anger all round. We are trying desperately to put the France match behind us.

The match itself was strange. We started reasonably well with the wind, but then it just went pear-shaped for a short period when the French helped themselves to two tries, as they are always capable of doing. Why did we fall apart? Why did we lose concentration? Why weren't we imposing ourselves on the French? We had home advantage and first use of a strong wind. Why weren't we showing the killer instinct?

France's first try from Christophe Dominici was a very well-worked set-piece backs' move which, watching the video afterwards, I could only admire, although I was cursing at the time. We would normally reckon to squeeze out an orthodox move like that, but this was France, remember, and they can be very sharp. They always run from deeper and at a slightly different angle from other teams, and they pass at a sharper angle. They give themselves a chance by creating more room for themselves.

The second try was sloppy, sloppy, sloppy by us – me in particular. Pathetic. We turned over the ball in the line-out and as we went from an attacking alignment to a defensive one I got myself horribly out of position. What the bloody hell was I doing? Benoit Baby, only their third choice but some player, sprinted in from sixty yards with our defence shredded. A very soft and annoying try to concede.

At half-time, 18–9 down and turning into the wind, I was still confident we could turn it around and win. We swapped penalties, and then, with about nine minutes remaining, our chance came. Freddie Michalak had come on and Fabien Pelous had just gone off to a thunderous ovation on the occasion of his 100th cap, and I just felt France had lost a little concentration, celebrating victory a tad prematurely with handshakes and high fives all round for Fabien. It was only 21–12. My mind went back to Leinster at Bath a few weeks back. Two tries, fourteen points, it can all happen very quickly. We were still well in it.

Even his best friend wouldn't describe Michalak as one of the world's best and bravest tacklers, and when we won some prime off-the-top line-out possession – a rarity on a day when we struggled against a very good French line-out – I really fancied it. ROG dummied inside to Maggsie, which held up Betsen and Nyanga, and suddenly it was backs on backs, me against Michalak. I had been waiting for this moment all match and the adrenalin kicked in. It was now or never if we were to have any chance of salvaging the game.

I buried my right hand in Freddie's face and pushed him off with a very satisfying hand-off. I lost my balance a little coming out of that and for a fraction of a second considered looking to off-load, but the act of regaining my balance seemed to sling-shot me and I was suddenly back to top speed and lasered in on the line. The full-back Laharrague was beaten all ends up, but the danger man was Cédric Heymans, who was cutting across to stop me.

He is a real gas merchant so I had to box clever here. First I headed straight for the corner to set him off on that angle and then cut right in at a sharp angle to score under the posts. It seemed very simple and preordained, and a little strange, because just for a second the crowd went very quiet. It had all looked so easy that you half thought there had to be a whistle for something and play would be called back. It never came and were back in the game: 21–19 with all to play for.

From that position we should have won – not that we necessarily deserved to, but since when has that prevented sides from stealing victories? Our golden opportunity came soon after as we again won some decent line-out ball. A dummy scissors in midfield and Kevin Maggs took the crash ball with only an off-balance Michalak to beat. Even though we were on half-way, it was a great opportunity, and we were all on the front foot poised to offer support. But Kevin couldn't hang on. There was no blame to be attached: it was a high-speed, high-risk move and fails as often it succeeds. I have dropped or spilled the ball much more than I care to remember in this Championship – it happens. But it was our big moment. There was no way back after it.

Maggsie, who is as passionate an Ireland player as you can get, was distraught in the corner of the changing room and obviously not going anywhere in a hurry, so I decided to go into the French dressing room to present their debutant and his opposite number, Benoit Baby, with my shirt on his debut. What happens on these occasions is that the debutant is allowed to keep his first national shirt and collect that of his opposite number. I will never forget how Daniel Herbert came in after my debut against Australia in 1999 and made a point of handing over his Aussie top and insisting I keep my green shirt on. A nice gesture, and I remember doing likewise when I played opposite Mike Tindall in his first Test.

With Maggsie upset I decided to do the honours with Baby. I was keen to find him anyway, to make sure there were no hard feelings after our little dust-up in the second half. Rugby is a pretty brutal physical sport, we all lose the plot sometimes and things happen that shouldn't. I won't condone foul play but at the same time I refuse to fall out personally with somebody off the pitch. I went in, congratulated Baby on a pretty stunning debut, handed over my shirt and insisted he kept his.

The citing officer – completely out of my control – has taken a different view, and Baby could be in trouble. If truth be told I am far from happy with my part in the incident and don't feel very clever about it. I was very hyped up – nothing seemed to be going for us and I was working overtime to try to spark something – and went in hard to clear out Sylvain Marconnet at a ruck.

Baby saw it and came flying in to administer a little retribution. At the time I thought I had been hit with a forearm or shoulder and it was only afterwards I realized it was a butt. I came up swinging wildly, I can't ever remember being so riled and angry, but fortunately for the both of us Serge Betsen stepped in between us and calmed things down. Neither of us fancied taking Serge on! Looking back, Baby should have got at least a yellow card there and then, and on another day I might have been joining him. I was lucky and trotted back feeling a bit guilty, as captain, at losing my cool. I was meant to be setting an example.

It took a real effort to stay positive for the TV and press interviews afterwards. I was hurting inside, but what the Ireland team and public wanted to hear was that it was still all to play for in Cardiff.

Still can't get my head around the match. If the two sides had put on some fresh kit after the final whistle and gone out there and kicked off again I know we would have won. We just had not given it our best shot, and I was bemused, irritated, depressed. Winning three or four games in a championship is not what we are about any more. This side should have been capable of winning the Grand Slam, and we had fallen short. I was bloody annoyed, and so was Eddie.

We gathered back at Mission Control last night. We were all completely out on our feet, and Eddie sensibly declared a two-day mini-break, time for some R and R. Not least for him. He looks exhausted and pretty down, like the rest of us.

Tuesday 15 March, City West

No point at all in flogging a dead horse. Yesterday there was golf for those who fancied it. Or the lounge lizards could indulge in a swim, sauna and massage. Or simply ten hours' sleep for those who needed it. I tried to combine a bit of everything!

Then there was a big team meal out at a local restaurant, and you could feel the spirit and enthusiasm coming back. It was good to experience. Ireland teams don't mope around for long. The smiles soon return, it's the way we are. Life is too short. You just have to learn how to handle defeat in this business, because no team ever goes on winning indefinitely. Losing to France was particularly galling, but we have lost before and bounced back well. We will survive and come strong again.

We are still copping a shed-load of serious criticism for the France defeat, much more than we expected. The fans and media are as disappointed as we are, and there is a lot of newspaper talk about the urgent need for this side to break up – at least in certain positions – and to start planning for the 2007 World Cup.

My first reaction is to get all defensive and reject everything they say. Give us a break, guys, we were only 21–19 down with seven or eight minutes to go and had every reason to believe we could pull through in a game that was only ever going to be decided by one score. France are a very good side – this team might even go on to be a great side – and we only just lost to them when not quite at full bore. In my book that means we must be a pretty good side as well. How many big games did England lose before they got everything right for the 2003 Grand Slam and World Cup? Let's go through them. Wales at Wembley in 1999, Scotland at Murrayfield in 2000 and Ireland in 2001 in the Foot and Mouth International, for starters. And it all went horribly wrong in the 1999 World Cup quarter-final against South Africa as well. But you can learn from these defeats, take the lessons on board, and finally go on to achieve big things. Ireland have been on an upward curve for four or five years, we have added something to our play every year and moved on after bad defeats such as England at Twickenham in 2002 and France in the 2003 World Cup.

We are the Triple Crown holders and we can still retain that title. Now is not the time for losing the faith, and I know I have made a really strong and logical argument . . . and yet deep down I share much of the frustration and maybe even the media's feeling that the team will soon have to undergo surgery, although that will not be my decision.

Our expectations and goals were high. It was only six weeks ago that I was telling everybody, 'Now is the time for Ireland, no more planning for the future, this is our season, this is the Championship we should win, this is the season we can truly aim for a Grand Slam.' We must live with the pressure, otherwise we are not the team we think we are.

Eddie has been stung by the media reaction – it has been a successful two or three years and criticism has not been the norm – but he was in feisty mood today and named exactly the same side that had started against the French. Firstly it was a vote of confidence in us and a sign that he was not going to make any knee-jerk selections. That has never been his style anyway. He is very big on loyalty. And secondly, to be frank, we don't have a whole load of options. Darce and Shaggy are out injured, so is Denis Leamy, and although Donncha O'Callaghan is champing at the bit for some action in the second row, there is no overwhelming case to be made for dropping either Malcolm O'Kelly, who has been outstanding for us, or Paul O'Connell, who has been very good, although they were both thoroughly tested against England and France.

We have to front up in Cardiff on Saturday. A packed Millennium Stadium, with Wales chasing their first Grand Slam in twenty-seven years, is not the place to be experimenting or throwing young players to the wolves. We are a good team, we have come a long way, so let's finish off this season together and, who knows, perhaps sneak off with another Triple Crown. I don't give a damn about spoiling the Welsh party, that's not why we are going to Cardiff. We will never win if we go in with that attitude. We have to turn up looking to achieve something for Ireland.

Wednesday 16 March, City West

Just heard Baby has got a month's ban for his butt on me – that means he will miss France's final game against Italy and Toulouse's Heineken Cup quarter-final against Northampton. Suppose a month is about right – it was there for everybody to see on the TV – but I still wish it had been dealt with properly at the time. Don't feel great about the whole incident. It could be tough on Baby. France, and Toulouse, have got so many quality backs that somebody is likely to come in and make a name for himself in the next month, and Baby could slip down the pecking order despite his brilliant debut against us.

Thursday 17 March, Hilton Hotel, Cardiff

We are always in the middle of the Six Nations come St Patrick's Day, so it's a long time since I celebrated properly with a jar and a day partying. Still, you are a long time retired, there will be plenty of time for that in years to come. We began the day at City West, trained in the morning – pretty well, actually – then flew to Cardiff this afternoon. The flash of cameras and lights was fairly amazing and you could sense straight away that this was no ordinary match. When we got to Cardiff it was buzzing – and it is still forty-eight hours before kick-off.

Sitting here in my hotel room, watching MTV as usual. A group of us have just got back from the cinema where we watched *Hitch*, a chick-flick about a dating agency with Will Smith doing his stuff. Very funny and quite romantic, an ideal film for a first date with the new lady in your life. Me? I had Donncha on one side and Frankie Sheahan on the other, both world-class messers with the concentration levels of a gnat. Good fun, though. The only way we can get through this week is to be relaxed and enjoy ourselves. Approach it in that fashion and we might just surprise a few people.

We know exactly how tough it is going to be on Saturday. History, fate, call it whatever you will, seems to be demanding a Wales victory. They have the entire nation behind them. Ireland will go well, though. The boys have recovered their self-confidence and poise. We are not out of the hunt yet.

Wales are a confidence team, always have been, and we have always tried to hit them hard and early to dent that swagger. Their skill levels are superb, and we see that every week in the Celtic League. At national level, though, they seem to have been on a roller-coaster for years now, with more downs than ups. Very rarely, except under Graham Henry, have they put a string of performances together. One setback or unlucky defeat and their heads would drop, and it could be another year before you saw the real Wales again. You always got the impression their players were walking on eggshells.

That all seems to have changed under Mike Ruddock. I know Mike well from when he was in charge at Leinster, indeed it was he who offered me my first ever contract. He is rock-solid and unflappable. He believes in attacking, running rugby in the old Welsh way. But he is a pragmatist and knows firstly that you have to build a pack to make that possible, and secondly that it can all go pear-shaped and you have to accept defeat sometimes without losing your confidence.

Wales had a good autumn, although they lost to South Africa and New Zealand. They played the brand of rugby they wanted and they have clearly got the Millennium Stadium crowd back on-side, which is a big factor. Their win over England first up in the Championship wasn't pretty, and to be fair it was a game they could easily have lost, but it was an absolutely massive psychological boost for them. Since then we have seen some spectacular rugby against Italy, France and then Scotland last week.

Wales are not unbeatable, though. We must fully test them mentally; perhaps they are still a bit vulnerable. We have given them two really big hidings in our last two games at Dublin and did them in cold blood two years ago in Cardiff when ROG popped over an injury-time dropped goal. The current bunch of Wales players have not got happy memories of playing Ireland.

Friday 18 March, Hilton Hotel

Temperature: 18 degrees. Cloud cover: none. Forecast: Cardiff is going to be a boiling cauldron tomorrow. Atmosphere: demob happy, end-of-termish. Relaxed 'walk-through' at the Millennium Stadium. Looking around, not for the first time, I was green with envy. What a stadium. It must be amazing playing here in front of the Welsh fans. If you can't play here you might as well give up. When are we going to get it sorted out in Dublin? Like everybody I love Lansdowne Road – the mighty roar, the intimacy and the tradition – but come on. This is the twenty-first century, prosperous times have arrived in Ireland, and we deserve better. The old place is falling apart. There are plans for a revamp by 2009, so we have got our fingers crossed, though the capacity (50,000) seems a little on the low side given that you could sell the international tickets two or three times over.

I read we might have to play our home games at Twickenham or Cardiff for three years if the rebuilding of Lansdowne Road goes ahead. Well, that would be grand, but why on earth aren't we automatically going to Croke Park, three miles across the way in Dublin and one of the finest stadia in the world? We are currently barred, along with the foot-

ballers, from Croke Park under Rule 42 of the GAA Con-
stitution. This is disappointing and perplexing: I thought sport
was all about uniting people, especially in a country like
Ireland, with its history. I shout and cheer for every single
Irish sportsman and woman who represents the nation.

When the Ireland rugby team has a big match, one in three
people throughout Ireland watch it live on the television,
including thousands and thousands of diehard GAA fans. I
know loads of them who come down to Lansdowne Road if
ever they can get a ticket. The rugby does a fair bit to lift the
morale of the country – in how many other sports can we
claim to rank in the top six in the world? Would it really hurt
anybody's sensibilities if we were allowed to play two or
three games every year at Croke while Lansdowne Road got
refitted? Can you just imagine what an incredible occasion it
would be if we fitted nearly 85,000 in for a Grand Slam
decider against, say, England? The entire nation could be
proud. I might be wrong here, but wasn't some of the money
used to finance Croke in the form of a government grant,
paid for by the taxpayers of Ireland, which will have included
many rugby and soccer fans? It doesn't seem quite right. We
are a small sporting nation, we should be sticking together.

There is a big meeting of all the GAA County Boards on
16 April to vote on the repeal of Rule 42. I am told the vote
could be close – it needs a two-thirds majority to be repealed
– but I am not holding my breath. Wouldn't it be unbelievable
if they gave us, the rugby players of Ireland, their support?
We wouldn't let them down. We would be proud, honoured
and just delighted to represent our country at their wonderful
stadium.

Cardiff is already crawling with supporters, or is it just that
everybody in Wales wears the national shirt these days? It's a

pre-match atmosphere the like of which I have never experienced before. A lot of Irish as well. The fans, who expected this to be our Grand Slam match, seem to have travelled over anyway. What with Cheltenham Festival finishing just down the road this afternoon, there is plenty of green to be seen. They must have bought the tickets in advance with the intention of making a big weekend of it. Another reason we must perform tomorrow. I think the Irish and Welsh supporters get on best of all. They all seem to be singing each other's songs, anyway.

Not feeling at all sleepy at present. Have been wide awake and busy all day. Might go for a wander around the hotel and see if any of the lads are up. I'm a great believer in not trying to sleep until I feel tired. I've had my massage with Willie, chewed the cud with him, collected my boots for tomorrow. It's lovely and peaceful in here. Expect it's carnage on the streets outside.

Sunday 20 March, Kehoe's Bar, Dublin

Actually, strictly speaking, en route to Kehoe's bar. Where have the last two months gone? That's another Six Nations done and dusted and as far as I am concerned it's the one that got away. Just flown in from Cardiff and we are heading off to Kehoe's for a good gargle and a laugh. It's become a tradition in recent years that we have a Championship winddown at Kehoe's on the last Sunday. Just the squad, or at least those of us who can linger in Dublin for the day and night. Plenty of beers and banter, a sort of unofficial debrief and basically a good time to make sure we all head off into what is left of the season feeling good about ourselves and about

Irish rugby. An old-fashioned rugby gathering, the kind we have too few of these days. It has been a very long haul this season. Feel absolutely wasted. It's like pricking a balloon the moment the Six Nations ends – your strength and energy just drain away and all the fatigue and the aches and pains of the last few months kick in. I recognize the signs now and don't worry about it too much, but for the first couple of years I thought I must be ill or something. Anyway these are the last coherent words I will be writing or uttering today. I am turning my mobile off for the next twenty-four hours. Should be back in the land of the living by Tuesday.

Tuesday 22 March, number 35

Chilling in the kitchen. MTV on. Just fixed myself a sand-wich. Great time Sunday, a good old end-of-Six-Nations party followed by a tramp around Dublin looking for some late music. Slept most of Monday, then trained with Leinster this morning and headed for my bed again. I am scribbling these notes at teatime now before heading for my bed yet again. I have a simple rule. If I am tired I go to bed and sleep. If I am not tired I am up and doing. There isn't much middle ground.

The Wales match. What can I say? It was an unbelievable occasion and the better side won. Congratulations, Wales, you took your Grand Slam in style. We kept you honest and the score respectable but it was your day.

As a rugby day it was unique and special. I was sitting next to David Humphreys on the coach as we made our short journey from the hotel and he said he had never known an atmosphere like it. He was right. There must have been hundreds of thousands of fans on the streets. There was no way even half of them could have got into the Millennium Stadium. Everybody was in their team's colours. Roads and streets didn't seem to exist, just streams of red-bedecked humanity ebbing and flowing.

Inside the ground it was extraordinary and the singing of the Welsh anthem the best ever. The WRU hired Charlotte Church and Katherine Jenkins – and Max Boyce helped out as well – but in truth you couldn't hear any of them, they might as well not have bothered. The crowd just took over and, as the old saying goes, you just couldn't hear yourself think.

We made a good enough start, ROG and Stephen Jones swapping penalties, and we thought we had weathered the storm when the key moment came, Gethin Jenkins charging down ROG's clearance kick and showing good control to dribble over for the try. It was a tough blow. I had just ripped the ball away off a Welsh player out near the touchline, and it was a good turnover ball, but Jenkins read the play perfectly. My immediate impression was that he had to be offside by a mile but having seen the replay he was at least two yards shy of the offside line and just showed incredible speed and anticipation. It goes to show how difficult these calls these are and that players on the pitch, and on the move, are usually in the worst position to make any worthwhile judgement.

It felt like an important moment, but an even more crucial incident came later in the half when we pulled off a cracking backs move, one of our favourites, with me flicking inside to Denis Hickie, who had tracked across from the other wing. Denis released Geordie perfectly and he got a great ball back inside to Girvan. It looked like a try for all money but somehow not one but three Welsh defenders – which tells you exactly how motivated for the game they were – got back to make the tackle. Mark Taylor was the guy who put the really decisive hit in. That was the moment we could have got back on level terms. After that we were in trouble.

I was getting plenty of stick from the Wales fans at this stage, courtesy of a little incident early in the half when Brett Cockbain was hanging on to my leg for dear life long after the ball had gone. He was preventing me from freeing myself and rejoining play. We were under pressure, play was continuing and I was needed in defence. I tried to shake my leg free not once but twice but still he clung on like a drowning man to a tree branch. This was ridiculous. He had to have it. I stamped down on his torso, still he clung on. I was getting really angry now so I stamped down a second time and this time he finally released me and I was allowed to go about my lawful business. Cockbain was totally out of order and he knew it, even if the crowd was going nuts – I accept it might not have looked pretty. The situation was no different from somebody deliberately lying offside at a ruck, preventing release of the ball. They know exactly what they are doing and the probable consequences of their actions. They are going to get a stud or two on their backs, plus a penalty against them, for their trouble.

On this occasion Cockbain got away lightly. I tried to clear my leg twice before resorting to plan B, and in the end it was me who got penalized. What was I meant to do? Stand by meekly while Wales raced past me and scored a try?

Still thought we were just about in it at half-time, but Wales played very well in the third quarter and pulled away steadily through Stephen Jones and a well-taken try from Kevin Morgan. At 31–13 down and the crowd baying we were looking at a drubbing and I was very proud how we crawled our way back to a bit of respectability. It was a very hot afternoon and a good opportunity to use a few of our replacements – Marcus Horan, David Humphreys and Donncha O'Callaghan. They all did very well, making the impact that you hope those on the bench will do. Marcus and Geordan Murphy both got over for tries. It wasn't really a taste of what could have been – we were still well beaten – but it meant we could leave Cardiff with our heads up.

The scenes after the final whistle were extraordinary. Tried to make sure I said well done to as many of the Welsh lads as I could, but really it was time to get off the pitch and let them enjoy their moment. By the time Max Boyce was starting up again it was definitely time to make ourselves scarce. You could still hear the singing deep down in our changing room.

The Welsh lads were good value afterwards – pretty humble about things – and it was impossible not to congratulate them sincerely, and wish them well. Went looking for Mike Ruddock to say well done but suddenly he was off doing hundreds of media interviews. At least I managed to say a sincere well done to him when the time came for my captain's speech at the reception.

Phoney Wars

Wednesday 23 March, number 35

Was sitting in my kitchen this morning sipping a coffee with the radio on when my ears pricked up. It was Clive Woodward speaking on what qualities he was looking for in his Lions captain. It must have been an old interview, because I know he's away abroad on holiday somewhere this week, but it was the first time I had heard it. 'I am not looking for a Martin Johnson clone but I want somebody with his single-minded approach. A leader, by example, on the field who will be his own man at all times and make his own decisions.' My pulse started racing. They were the exact same words I had used at one point during our little chat in Henley all those weeks ago. I wonder? Get a grip, Brian. Anybody with aspirations to the Lions captaincy would be thinking along those lines, surely. It's not exactly rocket science.

No good. I've been a basket case all day since hearing the words and can't settle to anything. Clive will have to make up his mind soon. The Six Nations is done and dusted. There is no reason to delay any more. Expect he's having a final ponder on holiday.

Thursday 24 March, number 35

Forgot yesterday to say a quick word about Brian O'Brien, the Ireland team manager who retired on Saturday after five years in charge. BrianO is possibly the most relaxed person on planet earth: he always looks like he has just come in from an afternoon's fishing. And canny as well. A real Limerick man! You could go up to BrianO and tell him you've committed murder or some other heinous crime and he wouldn't bat an eyelid. He is not high profile, he just quietly gets on with his job. Our previous manager, Donal Lenihan, was a former Ireland captain and Lion, a much more hands-on character who tended to dominate the press conferences and hammer home the official line. Brian is, sorry, was a behind-the-scenes facilitator, sorting out everything imaginable for the boys. A bit of a father figure as well. I will really miss his good humour.

Gave myself a bit of a talking-to over cornflakes this morning. It was stupid to get all excited about the Lions captaincy yesterday. Perhaps it's not meant to be, Clive would have been in touch by now. The main thing, if I get picked as a player, is to produce the rugby of my life.

Friday 25 March, Dublin

Trying to get back into the swing of things with Leinster, but it's difficult: the sense of anti-climax and sheer exhaustion when the Six Nations is over just knocks you back. I know a lot of fans feel pretty much the same themselves, so just imagine how the players suffer. The tournament has dominated my life since Christmas and suddenly it's just not

Evading World Player of the Year Schalk Burger in the November 2004
international versus South Africa – probably the best Ireland performance
I have been involved in.

After the high of beating South Africa, the win over Argentina was
a low – we played poorly and the Pumas' tactics were depressing.

Beach training at St Bart's with my mate Damien.

My 2004 hairstyle appears in its full autumn glory as I share
a light moment with Leinster teammates.

Leinster's Heineken Cup campaign got off to a good start, with
six consecutive victories – including home and away wins
against Bourgoin (*above*) and Bath (*below*).

We ground out a victory in our Six Nations opener against Italy, but I was gutted to injure my hamstring with the result already decided – next stop, the ice chambers of Poland.

Joking with Ronan O'Gara at a wintry Ireland training session.

Geordan sold the dummy and I brought home the bacon
– the decisive try in our win over England. Our smiles afterwards
indicate how satisfying the result was.

The modern rugby player spends a lot of time in the water,
soaking and rehabilitating sore muscles.

En route to a try against France at Lansdowne Road
– one of the few high points of a devastating defeat.

Serge Betsen helps keep me from getting into real trouble after
my dust-up with Benoit Baby (12). Afterwards I gave Baby
my shirt in recognition of a stunning debut.

there any more. Worse than that, it has finished on a down-beat note.

Really ought to play this weekend, our final run-out before the European Cup quarter-final against Leicester, but my hamstring has tightened up a bit and feels sore. Nothing drastic, but it is letting me know it's still there. To be honest I am amazed that it stood up so well over the last month or so.

Feel battered to hell and completely knackered. Intend to rein right back on the training and try to keep the fitness guys at bay a bit. They would have you working 24/7 given the chance! Rest is a big priority. Have got the quality work in the bank and the miles in my legs. My fitness is there, just waiting to be activated. I have pushed the hamstring hard and I think it needs a bit of natural healing time.

Some of the older international players have a bit of a chuckle when players of the modern era complain of being tired. OK, by old-time standards I haven't played a huge amount this season – let me see, four Celtic League matches so far, six Heineken Cup matches and eight Ireland inter-nationals. So what's that? Eighteen full-on games, although barring injury there is plenty more to come.

It is the intensity that has changed. In the old days there was one international in the autumn and four in the Championship and that was about it. The club matches wouldn't be the most demanding occasions ever. Now it's a minimum of eight internationals, and six Heineken Cup matches, which aren't far off Test matches in standard. Certainly we prepare all week for them like they were an international. And it's a cumulative thing as well. The last thirty months or so have been completely crazy – three Six Nations Championships; World Cup qualifiers including a flying visit to Siberia, of all places, to play Russia; the World Cup itself and all the warm-up internationals and training beforehand; three Heineken Cup campaigns; and three Celtic League Championships. I'm damned near on sixty Ireland caps now and I am just turned twenty-six. Every so often the body rebels, and you have to listen to your body.

Anyway, that's another Championship dead and buried. It should have been our best year since 1948 but it petered out into nothing much at all. The brain is gradually filing the special memories away after the madness of the last few weeks. You can't always take it in straight away. Spala, in a funny way, sticks in the mind. It was so bloody grim, austere and from another world, and we worked so hard. I pushed myself like I have rarely done before. It's amazing how much work you can get done when there is a specific target, i.e. saving my Six Nations, and absolutely no distractions. Thought the boys really turned it on either side of half-time against Scotland, enjoyed Geordie's magic little dummy to gift me a try against England and it felt great scoring against France, one of those you-can't-touch-me sort of moments. They are few and far between, but the funny thing is you always know a couple of seconds in advance that it is going to happen. You can feel the adrenalin surge and you are away.

What else? The depressing scene in the dressing room after the France match, when we realized that we had blown it and there could be no Grand Slam. The crowd scenes in Cardiff were very special – might not see anything like that again in my career – and finally a particularly pleasant session with the lads at Kehoe's, our only real kick-back all Championship. It's gone now, Brian. Move on.

Have got back with Glenda and am feeling much more relaxed with life and happy as a result. Everybody, it seems, wants to know all the ins and outs, but we are determined to maintain a discreet silence. Can't stop people asking and photographers trying to snatch photos of us together, but we will try to live our lives as a normal couple.

Saturday 26 March, number 35

Depressing, miserable, wet morning in Dublin. Bit delicate after a few beers with the lads last night. Was just enjoying brunch at a local café — I don't mind the cooking at home, it's the washing-up I can't abide with a bit of head on me — when a voice message from Clive Woodward flashed up on the mobile. Could I phone? No worries. I tried to reply but no luck: 'This number is unavailable, please try again later.' Then I sent a text message but I wasn't sure that had arrived either. Either his phone was playing up or mine. Waited for a while. What to do? Then a text arrived from Clive. He was trying to contact me, no joy so far but he would keep trying during the day. Waited a bit more. Fifteen minutes later and we still hadn't talked. God, this was purgatory. I kept going. Finally his phone rang.

'Hi, Brian, been trying to get you. How's things? We're on the beach in Barbados. It's absolutely gorgeous here, beautiful morning. Just been for an early-morning swim and walk on the beach. Fabulous.'

'Hi, Clive. Yeah, the sun is beating down here as well. Fantastic day. Very warm for the time of year. Dublin always looks a picture in the spring. Wouldn't be anywhere else in the world.'

'Oh,' he sounded just a tad disappointed. 'Anyway, just wanted to invite you, formally, to captain the Lions in New Zealand this summer. You are absolutely the right man for the job. Hoping very much you will accept.'

Bloody hell! Too right I will accept. I clenched my fist and punched the air for joy and started to shout the house down. The next minute or so is a complete blur. I've got no idea if Clive was talking to me or I was talking to him and absolutely no recollection of what was said. Gradually I came down off the ceiling and my head began to clear. Clive was outlining what happened from here on in.

'Right, we've got the big launch on Monday 11 April at the Hilton Hotel, Heathrow,' he said. 'Management and captain. You will have to come over on the Sunday night before and we will be doing the announcement live on Sky the next day about noon. It will all be a bit crazy, what with press and TV, but that's half the fun and you have got to get used to it. It will be a circus from now until mid-July.'

'I'm not sure I will be able to fit that in,' I said with what I thought was massive and hilarious irony. There was a long pause.

'What do you mean, can't fit it in?' came the slightly irritated reply from Sandy Lane beach or wherever.

Oh God. My appalling inability to deliver the funny line was backfiring on me again. We were back in the land of prawn sandwiches.

'Well, of course I suppose I could try to clear the diary,' I said, making one final effort to show I was joking.

Another long pause. This time-delay was doing my head in.

'Well, it would be nice if you could find time to pop in, Brian.'

It was time to move on quickly. Feeling a complete idiot, I stressed to Clive over and over again that I was ecstatic about the captaincy offer and would swim the Irish Sea and walk barefoot from Holyhead to Heathrow to accept what I consider to be the greatest honour in the game. We made a few arrangements about phone calls to discuss the squad and then he rang off.

Idiot. I made a real mess of that call. Wish we could do it again. I had deliberately talked my chances down in midweek so I wasn't really prepared for it. Still, I've got the next three months to redeem myself, on and off the field. I was just so nervous and happy and excited and relieved all at the same time. Oh well, the moment's gone now. Clive is used to dealing with nervous sportsmen, isn't he? He will have known how churned up I was and made allowances, I hope.

Clive swore me to secrecy for the next two weeks, but I was allowed to tell my folks, so I rang home and Mum answered. Dad was out. I knew from her tone of voice that she was delighted and proud. But she didn't go over the top. She is always the level-headed one, and I love her for it.

Friday 1 April, number 35

Clive has phoned a couple of times since the 'Barbados call'. Have been pleasantly surprised and impressed at how much input I am allowed to give towards the final squad selection. 'You will be the one leading the team, Brian, you have to be happy with all the troops around you,' was the gist of Clive's messages. So, with the exception of the front row, about which I know very little other than who is rated on the circuit by people whose views I respect, I chipped in with my thoughts and recommendations. Long phone call early this morning to go through his final shortlist of fifty-two or fifty-three, which has to be reduced to forty-four for next weekend. Probably thirty-five of those were definites, but even at this late stage there are plenty of either-ors. Everything still to play for this weekend.

Saturday 2 April, Lansdowne Road, Dublin

Got played off the park by Leicester in our Heineken Cup quarter-final this evening, never really in the game. From the moment Lewis Moody leapt high to claim the first kick-off the writing was on the wall. They were fantastic and blew us away. Really sharp, hard-edged performance from Leicester, which shows we are still a way off from being really competitive at the elite level. We got the usual accusations of Leinster bottling it, but that's unfair. When we lost to Perpignan in that semi, we were bad and did bottle it. But today Leicester were superb and we just weren't good enough to live with them. Their pack took a stranglehold on the game and we simply didn't have the ability to unlock their excellent defence. Leicester in full cry are a magnificent team. Just look at that pack. George Chuter, possibly the man of the match, is the only non-international. Very impressed with him – another later candidate for the Lions?

Ollie Smith had a sensational game in the centre in direct opposition to me. It's probably none of my business, but I'm completely gobsmacked that he hasn't been one of the first names down on the England team-sheet. Have not felt so pressurized and stretched by an opponent for a long while. Not only has he got great gas in attack but he's a tough customer and rattles into the tackles. A genuine revelation to me. He is a must for the Lions, surely, and if he does tour, even though I am captain, I will have to train and play like never before to hold him off.

Gordon D'Arcy got on for the last half hour and although it was way too late for him to influence the game he looked exceptionally fit and strong and pulled off one cracking tackle on big Martin Corry. It was important for him mentally to get just one small run before the Lions selection to show the powers that be that he is damned nearly there. Pleased for him. Have no doubts he will get the trip now.

Delighted to see Keith Gleeson back in the big time as well. This time last year Keith was the best openside in the Six Nations and was inked in to my prospective Lions XV. Then injury struck, and Ireland and Leinster have missed him desperately. He fetches and carries perfectly for a backline looking to attack and has been a huge loss. It's too late for the Lions now, but it will be great to have him back for Ireland even though he will have to fight hard to oust Johnny O'Connor. Look out for Shane Jennings as well. He's leaving Leinster for Tigers next season, and once the hard-edged Leicester ethos works through into his play he will be knocking on the Ireland door.

Geordan was in cracking form for Leicester, augurs well for the Lions. Leicester should beat Toulouse with something to spare in their semi-final and go on to lift the Heineken Cup.

Monday 4 April, number 35

Disappointed about Saturday, but no point dwelling – the Irish papers have predictably panned us, but so what? We weren't good enough this year and nothing can change that. Was just thinking about how good Ollie Smith was over a coffee in my kitchen this morning. His performance has really geed me up. I need to be stretched more. Looking back, I've had it too easy with Ireland. Within a couple of games of breaking into the side in 1999 I've been an 'automatic' choice, which is a great compliment, but you can end up in a comfort zone. Have tried hard to resist that feeling at all times, but it's inevitable given the circumstances. Now I feel very energized by the Lions selection and the fact that we have a clutch of world-class backs who are going to raise the bar at training and in games. From feeling lethargic and down just a fortnight ago after the Six Nations I am now determined to train like a maniac and have set myself all sorts of goals. Amazing how much of this game is mental. I'm buzzing now, can hardly sit still. Have chucked out all the junk food in my larder and bought up barrowloads of fruit and veg and healthy chicken and fish cutlets. When you up the training you have to up the food intake, but it has to be top-notch stuff. I'm determined to arrive in New Zealand in the very best shape of my life. I'm doing it for me and because, as captain, I want to set an example.

Wednesday 6 April, number 35

Declan Kidney has resigned as Leinster's coach and is moving back to Munster. Can't say I am surprised, got a whiff of his application for the Munster job last week and had a quick word with him. Believe, totally, his insistence that it is for family reasons and once he put his name into the hat he was always going to end up back with Munster, where he played a big part in their rise to prominence in the Heineken. Had a curious conversation with him, though. He wanted to talk about this season and the way ahead for the future, but I cut him short. 'You aren't going to be here, Declan, this is a completely pointless exercise.' Mentally he hadn't made the break from Leinster and he even offered to stay on for the rest of the season, but that was never on. We could end up playing Munster in the Celtic Cup over the next weeks. A fair few of the lads are really fed up with Declan. He's just finished a round of contract negotiations and laid some of the boys off. They are understandably up in arms and want a chance to press their case with the new appointment, whoever that might be. They have a fair point.

Bit of a mess, really. I have nothing personal against Declan, we go back to the U19 World Cup in France in 1998, when we won and he was the coach. He played a large part in that, convincing us that we were as good as any team in the world and hey, why shouldn't Ireland win? Thanks partly to those early lessons from Declan I have never run on to a rugby pitch feeling a lesser player than any opponent. But it hasn't worked out at Leinster, and perhaps a parting of the ways is for the best.

In all honesty I have scarcely learned a thing, technically, at Leinster for a couple of years now. My game hasn't progressed as I would have liked. I'm just honing old skills and maintaining fitness levels. What I would really like now is a brilliant and innovative technical coach, buzzing with new ideas and drills to help take my game to another level on a weekly basis. Somebody like Pat Howard at Leicester, although I know he is taken. It is with your club or province that you get the time to improve your game. When you meet up with Ireland it's all about establishing team pattern, perfecting moves, organizing. Apart from half an hour kicking every day there is no time to develop new aspects of your game. At a vital stage of my career – the really good years – I feel I have been treading water a little.

If I hadn't got the Lions to plot and plan for, all this Leinster business would be stressing me, coming off the back of

Ireland's disappointing finish to the season. But now I am just observing and noting without getting involved, although I am happy to offer my views at senior players' meetings and am determined to put in a storming end of the season on the pitch.

Saturday 9 April, London

Enjoying a quiet weekend sightseeing with Glenda in London. First time for everything. Clive phoned this evening with the final squad. I am thrilled. Every either-or selection has gone the way I hoped in my heart it would. That shows clearly that Clive and I are almost identical in our thinking and gut instincts, which I find very encouraging. Should help when the going gets tough. This is the squad we both want; now we have to make it work.

It is a very strong mix of experience and youth. There is talent everywhere I look. I feel immensely proud and humbled to be nominated as captain. I will dedicate the next three months, around the clock if need be, to ensuring that this is the most successful and enjoyable tour it can possibly be. This is the biggest thing to have happened in my life so far.

Clive ran through his plans to give Jonny another month to prove his fitness and form after all the injury problems, and ditto Mike Tindall and Phil Vickery, although they are extremely doubtful. Concur totally. Jonny is world class, a trump card. Does anybody seriously doubt he has a massive role to play if fit? More than anything in the world Graham Henry and the Kiwis would like the Lions to play safe and leave Jonny at home. So it's back to that golden rule – do what your opponents least want you to do. The Kiwis would be absolutely delighted if we left him at home. As far as I am concerned, Jonny, barring any other injury setbacks, is on the jumbo to Auckland.

Sunday 10 April, Hilton Hotel, Heathrow

Nearly midnight now and here I am locked in my hotel room watching the BBC's coverage of the US Masters from Augusta. Trying to stay calm before tomorrow's big announcement. Been here since midday under the most congenial house arrest, having been barred from venturing out lest the identity of the next Lions captain be leaked prematurely. Bit cloak-and-dagger, perhaps, but fun as well. I checked in at noon and was listed under the name of Marcus Jansa. Here we go again! One day Brendan O'Donovan, the next day Marcus Jansa. Sounds like a fast-talking American lawyer on a flying visit. Wonder if he knows Graham Delaney?

Louisa Cheetham, the press liaison officer for the Lions, calls in occasionally with the papers and some Lions 'stash' to wear tomorrow and generally makes sure I have everything I need. No worries. Done room-service lunch. Done room-service dinner. Dozed. Listened to some music. Watched the golf. It's the calm before the storm and not at all unpleasant. Very strange feeling – I suppose you would have to call it smug – knowing what the squad is for tomorrow. There's probably only half a dozen people in the world with that knowledge.

Watching Tiger Woods. Incredible last day from Augusta. To stay that cool under that sort of pressure. And not just to stay calm but to produce golf from another planet. It's an object lesson of what can be achieved if you want it badly enough. Very inspired.

Louisa says I could sneak down in twenty minutes or so to acquaint myself with the press room and podium for tomorrow, but the golf is too good – Chris DiMarco has come back brilliantly, he's another tough cookie who doesn't know when to quit – and I am too sleepy to move. Phone Dad instead. For the first time I can hear him getting a little emotional. He has been trying very hard to keep things under wraps, to help keep me calm, I suspect. There is no doubt that tomorrow will change my life for ever.

Tuesday 12 April, number 35

Morning after the night before. Didn't get a chance to write a word yesterday. Madness at Heathrow and then madness back home. And now I just don't know where to start. But it's important to try to get this down because these are the great days, I will never be here again.

The 'house arrest' continued right through to noon, so when I was smuggled into the press conference room/studio via the service lift and hidden behind a curtain I had no idea of what had been said before by Clive and others. Went on cold and have never felt so nervous in my life. Knees shaking, voice creaking, hands sweating, the works. Had decided the night before to do it without any autocue or prompt. Wanted to do it from the heart and start as I mean to go on. There won't be too many props around to help me, down in New Zealand, there will be press conferences and briefings most days, and I need to get comfortable in this environment. Think I have developed well over the last couple of years PR-wise with Ireland, but this is a different ball game, live TV, words being winged around the world almost before they are out of your mouth. Remind myself one last time not to attempt any humour!

So kept it simple and just told it how it was. How moved and emotional I felt about being selected as captain. How proud as well. What a torture it had been not being able to tell friends and family other than Mum and Dad. How determined I was to make this a successful and enjoyable tour. Then came a short Q and A. The journos had obviously fired all their best shots at Clive and were still digesting the apparent absence of Jonny, so there was an embarrassing pause and shuffling of papers. 'C'mon, guys, I'm not that boring surely,' I was muttering to myself. 'Please, just one question, make my day.' Eventually they came, a trickle rather than a torrent, but enough to allow me to express in a little more detail what it all meant to me. Somebody asked me about my memories of previous Lions tours and I had to admit they were virtually zero except for playing in Australia four years ago. 1997 registered a little and I love the Tour video that was released later with Keith Wood setting some sort of world record for swearing! 1993, the last time the Lions were in New Zealand, did not register all. 'I was much more interested in Mark Hughes and Manchester United in those days,' I told the press conference.

The real questioning came when the Sky transmission ended and we broke up for separate interviews for the next couple of hours. That gave me the opportunity to say everything that had been swilling around in my mind for the previous two weeks.

About 2.45 p.m. it was all done, and I realized I could still get the 3.30 back to Dublin if I dashed. Picked up my bag and glanced at my mobile as I ran to check in – forty-two text messages, fifteen voice messages and climbing – and made it with half a minute to spare. Just sat back in my seat bewildered by it all. Didn't have a book or a magazine or anything. Just sat there staring ahead blankly trying to make sense of everything.

Landed. What to do? Silly question. A party back at my place, of course. I've just been made captain of the Lions for God's sake! More people have probably walked on the moon than have been Lions tour captains. There were some very important people I needed to share this moment with. Close friends and family, say about twenty people. Stopped off at the off-licence at the end of my road, bought six bottles of champagne and forty-eight cans of beer, and headed home. Barry was already on the case and had got some grub organized and phoned a few people. The folks were on their way. Nice small do. Who was I kidding? Within no time there must have been forty of us and I sent out for reinforcements at the offie. Everybody, it seemed, has suddenly developed a liking for champagne. Dad very emotional. He can finally share his good news with friends and as a hard-core rugby man, steeped in the game's history, he is very excited as well as proud.

The Leinster lads arrived and there were a few tears of joy. Whatever happened to the stiff-upper-lip types who used to play the game? Denis Hickie, Shaggy and Darce have been on edge for a month or more, and certainly for the last week or so I had known their fate but couldn't say a word. I was delighted for them. Now we can all train and prepare for the big trip together. Shane Byrne and Malcolm O'Kelly as well. Four years ago Mal and I were the only Leinster players in the Lions squad. Now we can all egg each other on – the 'Leinster Six', as we have already been dubbed. ROG phoned, chuffed for him as well. He has been going through agonies. Some people had written him off, but Clive has taken the long-term view. ROG has been consistently good for four or five years with only the occasional dodgy perform-ance. He was the form fly-half in the autumn; Stephen Jones was the man in the Six Nations. And now the Lions. Who knows? Jonny comes into the equation as well if he makes the tour. One of them will emerge as first choice.

Quality over a period of time counts. It's the same criterion that applies to some of the England boys. Over the last five or six seasons they have had one below-par campaign – this season – but the rest of the time they have been top notch. You don't dispense with a proven player until there is clear evidence that his game is in terminal decline.

So lots of chat and phone calls and the party soon transferred into town, first to Flannery's pub, well known as a nurses' and policemen's haunt and therefore always lively on Monday night when the shifts switch over and they are on their first day off in a while. And then finally a club to ensure that every last moment of celebration had been squeezed out of the night. Was it ever.

Saturday 16 April, Glasgow

Good news from Northampton: Jonny came on for more than fifty minutes last night and went well, even though Newcastle lost narrowly. No problems, apparently, and kick-ing as well as ever. Pleased for him, and us! Good Leinster win at Glasgow today in the Celtic League, although we fell away in the second half. Very annoyed with myself for a bad missed tackle that let them back into the game. That's not the first time this season. It's a concentration thing. Must sharpen up. Leading by example is my captaincy style and I must not, under any circumstances, miss big tackles like that down in New Zealand.

And incredible news from back home. The GAA's Rule 42 has been overturned by the necessary two-thirds majority. Every chance, God willing, of playing our home games at Croke Park while Lansdowne Road is being rebuilt. Would give anything to play on that ground even once.

Sunday 17 April, Vale of Glamorgan Hotel, Cardiff

Air temperature: 16 degrees. Forecast: interesting times ahead. Atmosphere: first day at school. Gathering here tonight for a two-day Lions get-together, our only chance to meet up before 17 May, when it will be for real. Checked in and immediately found there was a mystery brown parcel waiting for me. I've heard about such things, and me a good Catholic boy! Ripped it open to discover a pristine Blackburn Rovers shirt signed by Mark Hughes. He had seen my little reference on the Sky programme and had included a heartfelt note from 'Sparky' wishing me all the best in New Zealand. Suddenly I was a twelve-year-old kid again and it seemed like Christmas: my all-time sporting hero taking the bother to send me his signed shirt. It will have pride of place on my wall when I get a games room sorted out back in Dublin. Brilliant start to proceedings.

The squad has been arriving from all parts. The Leicester boys and Richard Hill were hotfoot from what sounds like a roughhouse at Saracens. Martin Corry is a bit down, having been sent off following a fracas with Richard Hill, although you would never know anything had gone on between them.

Tough lads who know what the score is. Definitely the sort you want in the trenches when the going gets tough.

Only got here by the skin of my teeth myself. There was a major terrorist alert at Dublin airport – which later turned out to be a dummy security exercise – and the queue for the metal-detectors was stretching out on to the road. We waited for a while but eventually I decided it was time to try to exert a little influence. I went up to a policeman to explain our dilemma. Luckily he was a rugby fan and escorted us through to the boarding gate. Could feel some angry eyes staring into my back as we walked through! Would not like to have been late for my first official duties as Lions captain, though.

A lot of nervous tension in the camp. There are a few old Lions among us, but this is new territory for the vast majority of the squad. We are a long way from being a proper tour party yet, just a group of rugby players from four countries who have been kicking the living daylights out of each other for the last four years. Becoming a proper squad is the first priority, but it will take time.

Players from the respective countries socialize much less often than the public would think. Celtic League matches – you are in and out. Same also for the Six Nations most of the time. With the new compressed tournament you are invariably heading for home soon after the match. Sunday internationals are completely hopeless and even if you haven't got to move straight on to the next match the clubs and provinces are screaming blue murder and want you back on the training ground on Monday morning.

Bit of fun tonight filming a Sky tour trailer with Gavin Henson, Gordon Bulloch and a few others. Spent half an hour roaring like a Lion in front of the cameras. Actually, spent the first twenty minutes cracking up with laughter but eventually managed to compose myself and look suitably fierce and Lion-like. The technical wizards will now go to work and change our faces to those of lions and we should look completely terrifying by the time the trailer goes out. Not that Gavin needs much done to his mane of hair.

Wednesday 20 April, number 35

The two-day session in Wales was good value and went a long way to uniting us as a squad. Flew back with Denis Hickie, a sharp observer of life and all its foibles, who couldn't believe the transformation. He was extremely impressed with Clive Woodward and his methods.

There was no organized training, although I am so pumped up at the moment that I couldn't help putting in a couple of huge weight sessions early in the mornings. Am definitely a bit of an obsessive personality. Weights are my thing at the moment, I suppose, because I am trying to rest the legs a bit. Have to do it to the best of my ability and drive myself to the edge of my capability. Two or three weeks down the line and I will have had enough pumping iron and it will be back to speed work and sharpening up, but hopefully it will have served its purpose.

At the squad gathering, Bill Beaumont, the tour manager, and Clive got up and talked with a lot of emotion about the Lions. Ian McGeechan as well. Then a representative of each of the four countries – Martin Corry, Gordon Bulloch, Gareth Thomas and Paul O'Connell – said what the Lions tour meant to them and what they hoped to achieve. And then it was my turn, and for the first time in my life I really had given some thought to what I wanted to say. You don't get a second chance to make a first impression, and I wanted to kick my captaincy off in style. Very nervous, wanted to get this right.

My basic theme was that the only three Lions tours people remember in the modern era are '71, '74 and '97 – and the common denominator was that they were winning tours. The legends and stories always centre around the successful tours. Nobody I have met ever mentions 2001, and that was only four years ago. 1993? What happened then? 1983, 1977, 1968, 1966? That's no disrespect to those involved, and there were some awesome players. But Lions tours are judged on one criterion only. It was up to us, and it was within our power, to make 2005 one of the epic winning tours that rugby fans will talk about in fifty or 100 years' time. That was my ambition and motivation and hopefully others share it.

Backed this up with my own assertion that, after twenty-four hours celebrating my selection last week, I had knuckled down to training like I have never done before in my life. Earning selection for the Lions is wonderful, but it means nothing unless you wear the shirt with distinction and pride. Earning selection is just reaching the foothills safely, acclimatizing and then setting up base camp. Now we have to climb the mountain. The hard work has just begun. We have to train and play like never before to challenge for that Test place, and then those honoured to appear against the All Blacks have to raise their game again.

My second theme was that we must have fun and enjoy each other's company. For seven weeks we would be united as a squad, it was the only time we would ever be together, and let's make sure it was fun. Lions tours are the pinnacles of our careers, let's savour every moment. New Zealand is a seriously beautiful and wonderful country. I absolutely loved my one previous visit, it reminded me very much of Ireland with the relaxed pace of life, small population, villagey feel. The weather is about the same as well. Off the pitch New Zealand fans love their rugby and will always pass the time of day pleasantly. Their Test players are much more humble and sociable than their other southern hemisphere counterparts. Tana Umaga is a gem of a bloke, a warrior out there in the middle, a quiet soul brother and gentleman off the pitch. The Kiwis enjoy a song and a beer, and with the itinerary Clive has devised to keep rushing around to a minimum, there will be a chance to kick back and mix. Let's take the opportunity to prove that modern-day rugby players are not brainless robots and play the game with a smile. A few old-style school and hospital visits are very much back on the agenda. Pleased with the way I got my message over. At least there wasn't too much barracking, whoopee cushions or throwing of boiled sweets.

What else? Well, there was one exercise whereby each member had to interview, in depth, another squad member with a view to getting to know them. Myself and Shane Williams were paired off, and to my shame I knew very little about Shane, so it was an interesting experiment. I learned that he wasn't one of those wonder kids who star for national schoolboy and youth teams and that he had been forced to fight hard for everything he has achieved in this game. No fast-moving escalator to the top for Shane, just his own efforts and dedication. He used to be a scrum-half but was gradually moved out wide – always thought he had a nice pass on him for a wing! – and that immediately makes us blood brothers, because I started at scrum-half. I learned that he performs best and feels most comfortable when people show confidence in him and that that hadn't always been the case in a stop–start

Wales career. And finally I learned that he is absolutely mad for motorbikes and the whole motorhead scene – riding and generally drooling over them.

Who knows if any of this will come into play, but it might. If Shane is feeling a bit down on tour, or in a match, I know now that he responds best to the carrot rather than the stick. And if I bump into anything from the alien – to me – world of bikers and biking in New Zealand I will point Shane in that direction and, if I have time, go along with him and maybe even get kitted out in some leathers and give it a blast.

He put me on the spot a little when he asked about my most embarrassing moment and did I have any regrets? One answer sufficed for both questions. A couple of years back I did some advertisements for men's pants which resulted in some horrendous pics and posters of me in my underwear. Not a pretty sight, enough to put anybody off their breakfast. I contemplated briefly fleeing the country or pleading insanity and kept a very low profile for a couple of months before venturing into public again.

At one stage Clive and the entire management quit the room and the players were left to formulate our own Code of Conduct and tour objectives. Lawrence Dallaglio, a veteran of the successful '97 tour, had a big input here. At one stage we were discussing how to handle Test selection and the disappointment of those who didn't make it and also how to support players if they have a bad day at the office in any one game. The discussion set me thinking, and as we broke up Lawrence came over for a quiet word with me. He started talking quite earnestly on the subject, which was obviously one close to his heart.

'The message that we have to get over is that you can

never have a bad day for the Lions,' he said. 'These matches are among the most important of your life and you have to be at 100 per cent all the time. There can be no excuses. We have to be ruthless. Bad days at the office cannot happen when you are on a Lions tour. That's the philosophy we have to live by.'

It was a very good point, brilliantly made by somebody I respect. We have some big characters in this squad with their own strong personalities. Lawrence is going to be a huge factor in this tour. This is his third trip and he knows the ropes, even if his tour to Australia four years ago was ended abruptly through injury. I am looking forward to working with him and getting to know him much better.

After an hour or so we presented our findings to Clive. Every point was discussed in an adult way and every signifi-cant thing we wanted was included. The tour charter and other administrative bits and pieces are going to be printed up in a little booklet for all the players when we regather in Cardiff next month.

There were a couple of interesting bonding exercises. The first was the classic mosaic exercise whereby a big painting – this time with a Lions theme with all the national flags and emblems – is split into 100 squares and your team has to paint two or three of those squares. That of course means co-ordinating with the teams in charge of the squares bordering yours. It was very useful on that level, and there was also a large element of playground fun, getting covered in paint from head to toe. I have a horrible feeling the Lions committee will have to buy the hotel a new dining-room carpet after today, but the end product looked pretty good and we all posed for an individual picture alongside our painting. By the next morning one of the Lions backroom staff had all the pictures blown up and framed and signed by the entire party, a fantastic feel-good memento to take home before the tour had even begun.

The second exercise was just a straightforward cabaret after our team dinner. There were nine teams and we all had to do a turn. The world is divided into people who can do this kind of stuff and those who can't, and I undoubtedly belong to the latter. The trick then is to try to make a complete prat of yourself with some grace. Of the more skilled entertainers, none did better than Mr Ben Kay – M'Lud to his friends – who is one of the best mimics I have ever heard, clearly a loss to stage and screen. Bruce Forsyth, would you believe, is his star turn. He has quickly established himself as the leading contender to become Tour Judge – rather fitting, as I have learned this week that his late father was a very eminent High Court judge.

Finished off the evening with an enjoyable squad dinner. Everybody much more relaxed now. Nothing will bring us together better than training and playing together, and that's why I am delighted the Argentina game has been organized before we fly south, but this little gathering has accelerated the process.

Headed for home this afternoon after more weights and a measuring session for tour kit. Dashed for the taxi and had arrived at the airport when I realized I had left my bag with the hotel concierge. Damn. Would forget my head if it wasn't screwed on to my neck. Everything in the bag bar my passport – mobile phone, house keys, wallet. Oh well, I'll have to have it sent over to Dublin.

Thursday 21 April, number 35

Big weights session this morning. Still trying to match Denis on the upper-body stuff – he is stronger than he looks. Getting there, though. Then back to the house for a meeting and a cup of coffee with Paul Higgins, who will be supervising work on the house I am having built a wee bit down the road. The London Irish lock Bob Casey put me in touch with Paul, and I've had a great time working with the architect, Nevile Verdon, to design the dream house I've always wanted. I've managed to work in a hot tub on the back garden decking, and a games room for all the memorabilia I've accumulated in recent years, which is currently cluttering up every room in the house. Work is due to start in July and with a fair wind I could be moved in before Christmas.

It's time for a move, although I've been very happy here at number 35. For a long while I managed to keep the location under wraps, for which particular thanks to the many late-night taxi drivers who have got me home safely after big Dublin nights. But the secret is well and truly out now, and I've come back from a rugby weekend to find youngsters literally camping in my front garden waiting for me. If you look across the road there today you will see a couple of photographers hiding. I've got no front gate and no privacy here.

It has been a nice diversion getting this project under way over the past couple of months, something to occupy the grey matter. It has to be admitted I have very quickly become a house bore and a wannabee property tycoon. When I buy a newspaper these days I ignore the sports pages and go straight to the property section. I could barely tell you the rugby results from the weekend, but I know the price of a house in any part of Dublin to the nearest €25,000. My big dream now is to own one of those big houses down Herbert Road. They are gorgeous, but I'm a way short of that yet.

Cooked myself a healthy lunch of chicken, potatoes (no butter) and lorry loads of broccoli. Then an afternoon meeting with a few of the Leinster boys – Denis, Reggie Corrigan, Malcolm, Darce – about the way forward after Declan's departure. Made my point again about the need for a hard-core specialist coach who can take our individual games forward as well as putting an overall game plan into practice. We are a bit down about the Leinster situation but we must not be too hard on ourselves. We finished third in the Celtic League, albeit some way behind the Ospreys and Munster, and got bundled out of the quarter-finals of the Heineken by an outstanding side. There are some issues to be resolved, but it's not all doom and gloom. We must put in a big late-season effort and try to win the Celtic Cup.

Just phoned Mum: 'Would you like to come over for a meal tonight?'

'Grand, Mum. Perfect. I could do with a quiet night. Been really busy.'

'I'm doing chicken and potatoes and some veg, probably broccoli for a change. Nice and healthy. Would that suit?'

'That will be just lovely, Mum!'

Friday 22 April, number 35

Loads of media requests for interviews, and I am trying to help out wherever possible. That comes with the territory when you are appointed Lions captain. As with the Six Nations build-up, the important thing is to be passing on the same message and thoughts all the time, otherwise it looks like you are contradicting yourself or just bending with the wind. With the questions coming in and some fairly relaxing time on my hands, my thoughts about the tour have been crystallizing.

The strength of this tour party is definitely the hunger and the incredible competition for places. In 2001 we all knew what the Test team was from very early on, it's pointless denying it, and I was lucky to be among those earmarked early on for a Test start. That really is not the case now. All forty-four players getting on the plane at Heathrow on 25 May stand a chance of playing in the first Test. That means that training every day is going to be like a final trial in its intensity, and every second will count in the six games leading in to the first Test. That is so healthy and positive.

This squad is mad for it. The old England back-row of Lawrence Dallaglio, Richard Hill and Neil Back want – need – one last hurrah, one last pop at the greatest enemy of all before they can finally quit the international scene. Simon Taylor is fresh and roaring after a miserable year out with injury, Martyn Williams wants to take his game on another notch after a brilliant Six Nations. Paul O'Connell knows great things are expected of him, Malcolm O'Kelly is desperate to make up for a disappointing Lions tour in 2001, and Donncha O'Callaghan is a wild, tough boy who wants to make the big breakthrough. Danny Grewcock and Ben Kay are fantastic English warriors who have given all us Celts plenty of grief over the years, and they will be working overtime to ensure Ireland doesn't monopolize the second-row berths. Gethin Jenkins, Steve Thompson and Julian White are all new to Lions rugby. Gordon Bulloch is another fine player and experienced Lion who will relish getting away from the pressure of playing for an underperforming Scotland.

And so it goes on. Dwayne Peel wants to take his game up yet another notch and prove he is right up there with Rob Howley and George Gregan, the modern greats at scrum-half. Matt Dawson wants to end his Lions career with a bang. Chris Cusiter is desperate to show what he can do in a side going forward. Stephen Jones is in the form of his life and will fight hard to keep Jonny out. How big a challenge is that? ROG is up for this tour in a big way. Gavin Henson, Gordon D'Arcy, Will Greenwood, Tom Shanklin and Ollie Smith are sheer class at centre and the scrap for selection there is going to be unbelievable.

And Brian O'Driscoll? The Lions have so much talent at centre that he has to prove every second of every day – on the training pitch and in matches – that he is worthy of the automatic place that the captain is supposedly granted. And then, having hopefully cemented his place in the Test team, he must produce the best rugby of his life. And having produced the best rugby of his life, it is vital that, as captain, he somehow encourages everybody else to do the same.

Shane Williams has been told a hundred times that he is too small – but not by me or the Lions. No way. We think he is magic – I think he is magic – and want him to keep buzzing and stepping from start to finish and to give his opposite number nightmares.

Jason Robinson didn't really fire for England last season but my old roommate from 2001 is an unbelievable talent and he is a proud man who is never content with second best. Gareth Thomas is beside himself with joy at becoming a Lion after eighty-three Wales caps. Josh Lewsey is the most committed and honest player in the world and is almost exploding with pride. My mate Geordan Murphy wants to make up for missing out on the World Cup and I want to see him show the New Zealanders, the toughest critics in the world, what he can do. This is the stage on which to do it. A Lions tour to New Zealand, in my book, is the equal of the World Cup finals. I have never experienced so much energy and desire coming from a team or squad.

The management and coaching back-up is the greatest array of talent ever assembled for the Lions. The accumulated rugby brainpower and wisdom there is frightening. We will treat every single match like a Test. The twenty-two going into action will be fit like never before, rested, properly briefed and determined to play world-class rugby for eighty minutes. Nothing else is acceptable.

Monday 25 April, Dublin

Another round of interviews this morning. Paul Ackford of the *Sunday Telegraph* and Alex Spink from the *Mirror* flew over to catch me at a photo-shoot at Lansdowne Road. I make that ten major interviews now since the announcement on 11 April. Am trying to give them all my full attention but can't think of anything new or different to say. I must be a very boring subject. Beginning to fully appreciate the demands made on the likes of Martin Johnson and Keith Wood over their careers.

The Lions squad is picking up a few injuries, but that's inevitable I suppose. Chances are we will travel to New Zealand without two or three of the original party but we just have to stay in match shape. It is vital that we hit the tour running, there can be no coasting or hiding injured players while they recover. Iain Balshaw has a quadriceps problem from the Powergen Cup final, Lewis Moody aggravated knee ligaments against Toulouse – he was struggling down at our get-together in Wales and I was surprised to see him run out, although he would always run through a brick wall for Leicester – and Graham Rowntree has done something to his knee: word is he has popped a synovial membrane. Yesterday, Matt Stevens also strained knee ligaments for Bath against London Irish. Graham should definitely be OK, but the others sound a bit touch and go. Fingers crossed.

Surprised Leicester lost to Toulouse, but it could have been very different if Ollie Smith and Darren Morris had run in two golden opportunities in the first half and put them under real pressure. Toulouse are a class team, and if you cough up fourteen points and let them back in the game you are always going to struggle. Felt for Ollie Smith. Two days after hearing he had been picked for the Lions his father died suddenly and I can't imagine his mind has been dwelling too much on rugby recently. Not just surprised but also disappointed for Leicester. Would like to have seen Johnno and Neil Back finish their Leicester careers on a high – and I would feel a little happier if we had at least been knocked out by the eventual champions.

Friday 29 April, Lansdowne Road

Beat Glasgow to book a place in the semi-finals of the Celtic Cup. Typical Leinster performance, I'm afraid, brilliant in patches and then curiously inept. We came very close to letting Glasgow off the hook again. Very pleased indeed with one set-piece try we worked for Girvan. I ran straight at the defence and without changing my running angle or looking round just did a back-flip pass into space that I knew Gordon D'Arcy was running into. Worked an absolute treat and Girvan finished it off for a great score. Tried the same move against England for Ireland, but it didn't click that time. Gordon also scored a fine individual try and is looking fantastic at present. It could all work out brilliantly for him. He's as fresh as a daisy and hungry after missing virtually a year of international rugby.

Monday 2 May, number 35

Spent some of the afternoon going over the house plans again. I tend to lose myself totally in the task in hand; it's very relaxing in a strange sort of way. Early-morning weights session, more upper-body stuff. Feeling good. Catching up on Hickie! Also doing lots of stretching to keep my hamstrings healthy and strong. Some mild ribbing after Paul Ackford's feature in the *Sunday Telegraph* at the weekend drew attention to the size of my arse. Powerful hindquarters I prefer to call them! Paul was a bit surprised how strong and 'stocky' I was in the flesh, which after due consideration I will take as a compliment.

Power has always been a big part of my game. It's all pretty crowded in the midfield, and you rarely get a chance to make one of those classic outside breaks we all love – making that try for Geordie against Italy was an exception, and my try against France was a tad different, because the French defence had suddenly lost all shape and the space opened up. Most of the time you need to burst through the first tackle and then maybe the second before you can find a little space to operate and all over the world top centres are now seriously strong guys. Many of us could double up as props or hookers with another couple of stones.

Have decided that this is the last week of press and media for the time being. It's beginning to do my head in. I need a full ten days to myself before joining up in Cardiff on 17 May, when it will all start again, but at least we will have the Argentina match to talk about and there will be forty-three, maybe more, other players for the media to interview.

Trying desperately to fight that caged feeling I get in the last weeks before the Six Nations when I become very impatient and just want to get on with it. And I am finding the Leinster games very difficult. Yes, I want to do well because we could do with an uplifting end to the season. And yes, I know I need to keep playing because it is vital I am fully match fit and sharp from the moment we start training in earnest down in Cardiff. But there is no mental trick or exercise in existence that can disguise the fact that nothing matters now except the Lions.

The Lions management has sent out some fitness guidelines and targets, and the Leinster Six have been having some fun trying them out. I don't believe there is a rugby player in the world who could attain all the required levels, but we are busting a gut to get there. That, I suspect, is the whole reason they have been put in place.

Clive phoned to compare notes and pass on a few thoughts. The news about Jonny is still encouraging: he played the full eighty minutes for Newcastle against London Irish on Saturday, kicked six goals and made their try. Looks very promising, but Clive wants to see one more eighty-minute performance – they have a wildcard game at Gloucester on Sunday – before making a definitive decision. Strikes me as all very sensible and sound thinking.

Leinster have got Munster at Lansdowne Road on Saturday in the Celtic semi-final. Suspect this might be the one match that means something before the Lions. Lots of long-standing rivalries and old scores to be settled, notably our New Year's Day defeat down in Cork. God, that seems a long time ago.

Sunday 8 May, Lansdowne Road

Leinster beaten by Munster in the last minute by an Anthony Foley try. Just about sums up a pretty average season for us. It was always going to be close, and in fairness we were unlucky. We just had our noses in front when poor Dave Holwell got sent off for an absolute nothing incident five minutes from the end. Bad decision and one that unhinged us at a key moment. Hate losing to Munster under any circumstance, and it was the usual niggly encounter between the two of us, but won't shed too many tears on this occasion. Have been finding it difficult to concentrate fully on Leinster with so many Lions thoughts in my head. Make a little promise to myself to try even harder to make things happen for Leinster next year and move on. It's Lions all the way now.

Fantastic news from Kingsholm: Jonny has come through OK against Gloucester and is on the tour. Feel a real surge of optimism and confidence. He's the complete fly-half. If Jonny is in the Test team that's brilliant – and anyone who can keep him out of the team, like Stephen Jones, will have to be playing incredible rugby. Either way the Lions will be the winners.

Big fuss over in England with the England coaches and staff on the Lions tour receiving a letter asking them to log any time over fifteen minutes they spend on Lions business

before their contract officially begins on 17 May. How petty
is that? Clive was outraged to start off with but then decided
to see it as the ridiculous gesture it is. Not worth wasting a
single second of energy on. We have bigger battles to fight.

Monday 9 May, number 35

Dreadful, dreadful day. The Leinster team doctor Jim
McShane and his wife Dolores suffered a terrible tragedy on
Saturday when their young son, Teddy, aged just three I
believe, was killed in a drowning accident. Today was the
funeral in Dun Laoghaire, with everybody from Leinster
attending. It was absolutely heartbreaking to see the little
white coffin carried down the aisle for the service before the
burial. Not one of us could hold back the tears. Jim and
Dolores are two of the nicest people you can ever meet and
they are, of course, absolutely devastated. Can't think of
anything more to write or say on this subject.

We had planned a big send-off at Kiely's in Donnybrook
tonight. David Holwell – a very fine player and top bloke who
has been a major success despite our difficulties at Leinster this
season – is going back home to New Zealand. Shane Jennings
and now Leo Cullen are away to Leicester, and Victor
Costello is hanging up his boots. Given the circumstances,
however, none of us had any heart for it. A couple of quick
pints and a promise to meet up again in happier times sufficed.

Saturday 14 May, number 35

Rushing around doing a million things before heading away to Cardiff early on Monday morning. Used the week off productively. Felt fully recovered from Sunday's match by Tuesday, which is a good sign, so trained hard Tuesday to Thursday – fair bit of speed work – and then clocked off for three days altogether. The body deserves a break. I've just been bundling together all the good-luck cards; my mum insists I should keep them in a scrapbook. The response has been fantastic. The Taoiseach sent a letter of of congratulatons, while former Lions captain Ronnie Dawson wrote a nice letter, as did Tom Kiernan. Like most of the current players I possibly stand accused of underestimating the older generation, the greybeards. The fact is that they were once twenty-six themselves – fit and fast with the world at their feet. They have done it all, toured the great rugby countries and taken on the legends of the game. They deserve our total respect and I was extremely touched that they took the bother to write, rather than just pass on good wishes. Old schoolmasters from Blackrock have been in touch, and a couple of old classmates I haven't heard of since the day we left. All sorts.

Sunday 15 May, number 35

Very nervous today. The tour is upon us and it hit me like a ton of bricks, the only time in the entire build-up so far. This is it. It's not so much saying goodbye to loved ones and friends, though that always tugs at the heartstrings. I am well used to spending time away on tour, and in any case most of the family, not to mention scores of rugby friends and mates from all over Ireland, will be down in New Zealand at various times during the tour. Mum, Dad, my two sisters, Jules's fiancé Tomás and Glenda are all coming down for the Test fortnight.

No, it was something else altogether today and rather strange. I felt like I was moving out of the cosy comfort zone in which I have spent the last twenty-six years. When you play with Ireland, although we aim high and have done well recently, expectations are still realistic. It is always possible to claim mitigating circumstances. But not with the Lions, I suspect. In the next two months or so I will be judged across Britain and Ireland solely on whether the Lions are successful or not. The 2005 tour will either join the immortal tours I spoke of at our first gathering, or we will be 'failures', the harsh verdict on our efforts four years ago. There is no in between. Captaining the Lions is a huge responsibility which I have tried not to dwell on overmuch. There are a hundred and one things to do every day, and all the time I am trying to say the right things and not let anybody down.

Have just had a cuppa and given myself a little pep talk. Don't look too far to the future, Brian. Don't try to anticipate problems and scenarios. You can never be totally prepared, so rely on your instincts. Don't be too rigid in what you say at press functions. Listen properly to the questions. If a problem arises, deal with it. Don't play the games in your head before you have even kicked off. Prepare, but then let it happen naturally. Work hard, wake up each morning with a clear conscience, treat each day on its merits and do your best. It will be bloody hard in New Zealand but you can only really take pleasure from an achievement if you have had to work for it.

Feel much better for that exercise.

Monday 16 May, *Vale of Glamorgan Hotel*

Nine p.m. and I'm nearly ready for my bed after a hectic final round of sponsors' calls. Checked into the Vale early on, then went up to London for a TAG shoot, back to Cardiff for some work with Gillette and finally back to the Vale to link up with Adidas. All finished now. The rugby can start in earnest. My nerves and self-doubts of yesterday have gone. Haven't had time to worry or ponder; I am always at my best when busy. Just bumped into Jonny in the lobby. Great to see him again. Very reassuring. It's been a long haul, but I am delighted he made the tour. He looks very fit and healthy and is obviously a man intent on making up for lost time.

Tuesday 17 May, *Vale of Glamorgan Hotel*

Lazy start after twelve solid hours of sleep. I'm storing it away like a camel for the hard times ahead. Players arriving from all parts, this time with real excitement and anticipation on their faces. Mainly admin today, collecting all our gear and official uniform, signing various insurance forms and then autographing a stack of balls and posters and stuff. Just heard confirmation that Iain Balshaw has had to withdraw with his quadricep injury. Very tough on Iain, who has got his career back on track after a couple of injury-plagued years. Shudder just a bit. We are all one hamstring tear or twisted knee away from disaster this week. Fingers crossed for everybody. This is a very difficult time. Some people have criticized the Lions for organizing the Pumas game, but in my experience preparing for a Test makes training that much more concentrated and sharp. If we were just looking at a week's full-contact training it might all get a bit fractious as individuals try to score points in the race for a Test place. I want that edge present in everything we do in New Zealand – it's exactly how we can raise our levels to new heights – but I am happy that this week training is more tempered and match-specific.

As one door closes another opens, and Iain's misfortune is definitely a big break for Sale's Mark Cueto. By common consent Mark was the unluckiest player not to make the original party: he has been scoring tries for fun over the past couple of seasons, a natural finisher who moved up to international rugby without batting an eyelid. I've seen plenty of him during Leinster's games against Sale, and though it all got a bit controversial at the time, I was deeply impressed with how he took the 'try that never was' for England against Ireland in February. Most impressive of all has been how he reacted to not making the original party on 11 April. Rather than get down on himself or whinge he has been on fire, determined to prove everybody wrong. He has just travelled down from Sale to do the admin stuff before returning to prepare for their European Challenge Cup final on Saturday. A very happy bunny indeed. Mark is on a roll, fancy he might figure in the Test series at some stage.

Wednesday 18 May, Vale of Glamorgan Hotel

Big day. We announced our first Lions team of the tour for our game against Argentina on Monday night. Clive pulled me aside a couple of weeks back and said he definitely wanted me leading the Lions on to the field in Rotorua against Bay of Plenty on 4 June, and, that being the case, I wouldn't be involved in any way against Argentina. Grand. Happy enough with that, though my inclination is always to play. It's the classic sportsman's insecurity. What if the guy coming in has a stormer? It's going to be a long tour, though, and, as captain, actually getting to New Zealand is an important part of it.

Michael Owen is going to captain first up and he will be thrilled: the Wales Grand Slam captain leading the Lions on at the Millennium. There are plenty of Lions unavailable for selection. Gareth Thomas is playing in the Heineken Cup final and Stephen Jones for his club in France. The five Sale boys are in the Challenge Cup final, we can't really select Neil Back given his pending disciplinary hearing, and others like Richard Hill are resting minor knocks. Don't think too much can be read into the selections.

The big news is the return of Jonny Wilkinson, whom Clive had always hoped to play in this game to get him back in the international groove. He has been ripping it in training and looks damned near back to his best. I'd forgotten what a pleasure it is to train alongside him and how he likes to call the shots and boss a situation. It will be great to see him back in action.

Broke off in the afternoon to talk to another of my all-time sporting heroes, Roy Keane, the Manchester United captain and former Ireland captain. This job certainly has its perks.

First chance I have ever had to talk to him properly. United are staying at the hotel ahead of the FA Cup final against Arsenal on Saturday and Roy seemed in great form when we chatted. He asked me how I was handling the whole captaincy thing, which was a very good question, actually. How am I doing? Results on the field in New Zealand will ultimately decide how people look on me, but so far it's going OK. Captaining the Lions is a full-time occupation, you are in-volved in all the squad and management meetings, and you are on show 24/7 around the hotel. And of course every media organization wants their twenty minutes. Roy has been there and got the T-shirt and gave a chuckle of understanding when I started painting the picture. He has become a bit of a rugby fan and was at Lansdowne Road for the England game. He is very proud that Ireland have eleven players in the Lions squad. We left with a handshake and he told me just to be my own man and above all else to look after myself and make sure I was playing at the top of my game. That was the best contribution I could make as captain. As we parted Roy was saying he had to serve a short ban after the FA Cup final and was planning some quality training before Ireland's World Cup qualifier against the Faroe Islands. Then it was a two-week family holiday and back to training with United and a pre-season tour. These guys get even less rest than us.

Felt a twinge in my hip flexor this afternoon after giving it heaps in the gym this morning doing a new set of exercises Dave Reddin has introduced me to. It was amazing to see the Lions backroom team click into action. I mentioned it first to Gary O'Driscoll – a second cousin of mine who is a GP in Manchester – who works as a team doctor along with the head doctor, James Robson, a Lions veteran of four tours now.

Gary examined me and then sent me down to the physio

room, where no fewer than four experts are on 24-hour call, working out a rota system among themselves. This time Bob Stewart and Stuart Barton were in residence and, after a quick conference among themselves, Barty announced he had a 'little trick' that would sort the problem out. And with that he grabbed my ankle with one hand and applied heavy pressure to the affected hip and butt with the other. One quick twist of the ankle seemed to clear the problem. They are also going to use a special strapping for the next couple of days in training to help the problem.

Thursday 19 May, Vale of Glamorgan Hotel

A few glum faces last night when we learned Neil Back had been handed a month's suspension for punching Joe Worsley in the Zurich Championship play-off against Wasps last Saturday. Seems harsh – we were hoping for two weeks – but we've decided not to appeal. We want no distractions at present and an appeal can't be heard until Monday, which would detract from the Argentina game. We want to concentrate on the rugby.

It's tough on Neil, but he has got to react positively and show us again what a consummate professional he is. Effectively he will now have one provincial match in New Zealand, against Wellington on 14 June, to mount a Test challenge. That would be daunting for most players but he is so fit and so good at preparing himself for a big game. If anybody can do it, Neil can. In the meantime he must help set the standards in training. We must keep him feeling involved. Clive asked him to do the water bottles on Monday, keeping him in the changing-room environment and on the pitch.

Friday 20 May, Vale of Glamorgan Hotel

Another good day's training, quality rather than quantity. It's invigorating to be working amongst so much talent. I feel on my mettle. Its not sufficient being simply 'good' at training any more. I have to be outstanding all the time. If everybody picks up on that attitude I am making a big contribution as captain. Off the training pitch I am making a conscious effort not to linger in my room listening to music. As captain I want to be visible and accessible, so I wander around the hotel lobby shooting the breeze with all the lads, ordering up gallons of tea and coffee and generally getting to know them a bit better and making sure they have no worries.

Beginning to relax. This afternoon I was hit by a surge of confidence. God, we have got some great players in the squad. If all forty-five play to their best – no, let's not be greedy, let's say if thirty play at their very best – this could be one of the all-time great teams. Why not? I expect other Lions squads have travelled with the same thought. It's unlocking all that magic and performing under great pressure against a world-class side on their own patch that is the challenge.

Saturday 21 May, Vale of Glamorgan Hotel

Temperature: 12 degrees. Forecast: a glorious afternoon for all United supporters. Atmosphere: holiday mood. It's FA Cup final day, and we've all got tickets. Very excited. I haven't watched United in the flesh for eighteen months now, which is a shocking admission from someone who considers himself a true fan. And I have never been to an FA

Cup final before. We are going to be in the VIP seats, but I will be wearing the colours with pride and shouting my head off. Gareth Jenkins, the Llanelli coach who is with the party, is a big Gooner, and we have been circling each other warily all morning since breakfast, trying to think of something witty or clever to say. We end up making vaguely silly faces at each other. Arsenal–Man U always has an edge to it. Great relaxing day in prospect, though. Nothing on the agenda for those not playing on Monday except R and R and watching the Cup final. The team for the Argentina game had a session this morning, and Malcolm O'Kelly pulled up with a muscle tear in his stomach and Simon Taylor felt a hamstring. Nothing too serious, I hope, but both were immediately withdrawn from the match. Martin Corry and Donncha O'Callaghan were drafted in to start with Lawrence Dallaglio and Ben Kay coming on to the bench.

The coaches – you need two when this Lions squad travel en bloc – have arrived, and a police escort has been organized, so I had better not keep anybody waiting. Better sign off now. Prediction? United 3–1 – no, that's a bit greedy. Make it 2–1.

Sunday 22 May, Vale of Glamorgan Hotel

Gutted, absolutely gutted. Can't believe we lost that game yesterday. United played Arsenal off the park, 3–0 would have been a just score. How did it ever get to penalties? Fair play to Arsenal, though. Having somehow made it through normal time and extra time, their penalties were stunning. No keeper could have got close. Thought Ashley Cole's was the best of the lot. Full of admiration for sportsmen who can perform under pressure like that.

Apart from the result, which really knocked me back for an hour or so, it was one of the great days. The match itself was probably the best 0–0 draw I ever saw. The Millennium Stadium was unbelievable, I have never heard noise like it. Football crowds are definitely noisier than rugby. Must be the tribal chanting thing and the fact that each side has about the same number of fans shouting for them. Rugby crowds ebb and flow much more. They can be incredibly noisy for short periods – even louder than football – as play reaches a crescendo and you can see a try is about to be scored, but then it peters out and there are long periods of relative silence. Let's face it, in some matches it can be five minutes before there is any action worth cheering!

Had a spectacular view on half-way, first tier, row one, and not for the first time I realized what brilliant athletes the football boys are. TV does them no justice at all. When you watch football on the telly it's like moving chess pieces around and you get no impression of physical effort and speed, the 60–70-yard bursts players put in just to shadow an opposition player or to provide an option down the wing. My hero Roy Keane had a cracking game. He is some competitor. Would have made a brilliant back for Ireland if he had started playing with an oval ball first. I wouldn't have classed myself as a Darren Fletcher fan before yesterday, but seeing him in the flesh has changed my view. What an engine, what a worker. He makes it possible for others.

Nipped out quickly for the toilet at half-time and suddenly became aware of a presence beside me as I did the necessary at the urinal. It was Ray, one of our designated security guys and ex-SAS, pretending to have a pee.

'Don't worry, Brian lad, I don't make a habit of this, mate, just ignore me, I'm not here,' said Ray out of the side of his mouth. 'Just making sure there's no bother. Better safe than sorry.'

Very professional, very unobtrusive. I'm just not used to this celebrity thing. There I was, an obvious United fan and a bit of a public face, in a toilet heaving with Arsenal supporters on Cup final day. I didn't sense an ounce of trouble, everybody was absolutely fine and there were even a few friendly nods of recognition, but it's exactly the sort of scenario in which a fan, perhaps having had one drink too many, might have taken a swing. Ray had spotted the potential well in advance and in true SAS fashion was ahead of the game.

Was pretty glum for a while after the match but soon cheered up on the coach journey back to our hotel. After dinner Clive gave me the nod to go back into town later with a few of the lads who were playing no part in Monday's game. It would be our last chance to relax and have a jar for at least a fortnight.

So we headed into the night – myself, Richard Hill, Matt Dawson, Josh Lewsey, Will Greenwood, Matt Stevens, Paul O'Connell and a few Welsh lads like Dwayne Peel, Martyn Williams and Tom Shanklin, who are of course the uncrowned Kings of Cardiff after their recent Grand Slam.

That's when we eventually got there. Three miles down the road from the hotel and our Range Rover suddenly ground to a halt, rather dramatically. Ray and Neil, another SAS veteran, quickly leaped out, but we didn't seem to be under enemy fire. POC and Matt jumped out and pushed the vehicle to the side of the road – excellent extra training for the boys. Our minders checked the vehicle from front to back and inside out before eventually concluding that . . . we had run out of petrol. Red faces all round from Hereford's finest, but no worries, a replacement was quickly summoned and we continued on our way.

Cardiff is a full-on rugby town, and it was brilliant mixing and yarning with genuine fans. You could feel an amazing enthusiasm for the tour. As the night wore on, however, there were a few who, inevitably, wanted to have a pop and see exactly how tough we were, etc., etc. On these occasions I usually count to ten and try to be polite or just move away, but it can be very difficult. Ray and Neil made life very easy for us, though. With their sixth sense for trouble they spotted the difficult customers a long way off and intercepted them perfectly. Politely at first, but firmly and expertly if the punter persisted.

'Don't be worrying yourself, Brian, crack on with the lads, make sure they have a good night,' Ray told me. 'Let me and Neil be rude for you, it's what we are paid for.' Top class.

Despite the heaving crowds, we were waved to the front of every queue and had a cracking evening. My abiding memory of the night was late on when Josh Lewsey downed a pint of lager in about four gulps and leant over conspiratorially: 'You know, Brian, it's all very well painting pretty pictures and doing cabaret turns, but this is the best kind of team bonding known to man!'

True enough. In vino veritas. You really get to know your colleagues over a pint. As the night wore on, Shanks, for example, quickly emerged as a gas character. Nearly as funny as Ben Kay.

Feel superb today, very together and happy. Have sensed the entire squad coming together over the last forty-eight hours. In fairness it can only happen when you are finally together with a real purpose. Until that point everything is, inevitably, a little artificial.

Been listening to the little iPod we have all been given, which includes a favourite song from every member of the party. Lots of U2. Geordan has opted for one of Lucie's songs. 'There's nice,' as they say down here. Will Greenwood is a big Neil Diamond fan. Me? I went for my favourite dance track, 'Children' by Robert Miles. Notice Alastair Campbell has opted for 'The Winner Takes It All' by Abba. On further investigation he tells me that when Labour won the 1997 General Election he turned on the radio the next morning and that was the first tune he heard. Good story. Could even be true.

Popped into the TV lounge a minute ago and chef Dave Campbell was fast asleep on the settee 'watching' the football highlights. Dave has got to be the hardest-working member of the party, up from dawn to late at night preparing the best and most nutritious grub I have ever tasted. He has perfected the art of making that which is good for you actually look tasty and appetizing. There was a bit of an eye-opener for me at dinner last night when we got back from the football. The twenty-two involved in the Argentina match were served up a nice big square of chocolate to go with their dessert. Our diets have been worked out to the final fifty calories or so, and Dave keeps a few calories up his sleeve to 'pamper' the match players as the game approaches. Talk about attention to detail. Apparently it's an England thing. No wonder they won the World Cup.

Time for a massage with Stuart Barton, our chief masseur and one of the best I've ever known. Everybody should have a Barty in their life. And then a meeting with Clive. Everything in the garden rosy. Still can't believe United lost, though.

Monday 23 May, Vale of Glamorgan Hotel

Morning: relaxing for an hour before heading off down to the Millennium Stadium. Trained hard this morning with the players who are not involved tonight. A win has to be our priority against Argentina, followed by a good performance, but strictly in that order. Was surprised to read some of the press, notably Paul Ackford, writing off the Pumas and ridiculing the fixture. When have you ever seen a non-competitive Pumas side in the last decade? We in Ireland know exactly how tough they always are. They can field two or three packs that can make life difficult for any international side and have some talented young backs coming through. My Leinster team-mate Felipe Contepomi tells me he won't even be doing the goal-kicking tonight, a fella by the name of Federico Todeschin who plays at Béziers in France is considered the current hotshot. Must be pretty good because Felipe is a 75 per cent international kicker himself. Let's look at this logically. The Lions, after just four sessions together, are playing a national side ranked seventh or eighth in the world. The Pumas spend their life on the road and are well used to gathering and playing at short notice. Argentina are without a host of players but still have eleven full caps, I believe, and the rest are extremely promising newcomers. A tricky encounter, I would say, one of the tougher tour openers in recent Lions' history. It's what we need, though. It will accelerate the team-building, and training will go up a couple of notches when we have the tapes to look at.

Tuesday 24 May, Vale of Glamorgan Hotel

Thank God for Jonny! He clinched a draw with an injury-time penalty to make it 25–25. Disappointed but not too downcast. Opening results are largely meaningless. We put over 100 on a hapless Western Australia in 2001, but the tour ultimately ended in failure. The 1971 Lions lost their first warm-up game against Queensland – I've been reading up on my Lions history since being appointed captain – and then scraped through against New South Wales before going on to great things in New Zealand. In any case I fully expected the Pumas to be awkward and spirited. What I didn't reckon on, to be frank, was the very high quality of their defence. From that point of view it was a brilliant workout. We were asked questions for the entire eighty minutes, ninety if you include the long period of injury time.

We were very apprehensive approaching kick-off. Just four of our starting side had ever experienced a Lions game before – Jonny, Graham Rowntree, Danny Grewcock and Martin Corry – and everybody seemed excited and over-anxious. What with that and the game being just forty-eight hours before our departure and everybody deep down hoping they wouldn't get badly injured, the nerves were jangling and it was reflected in our play.

The positives? Well, we didn't lose. Jonny is clearly back in the groove, and Geordan Murphy and Shane Williams had some very good moments. Ollie Smith took his try very well and looked sharp. Generally, though, it's just the feeling that the talking has stopped and now we can get on with doing what we do best. We have got loads to work on in training now, and I expect things to really start cranking up next week.

Contemplating defeat in the Ireland dressing room after the France match.

Tackling Tom Shanklin of Wales as they won the Grand Slam in Cardiff.

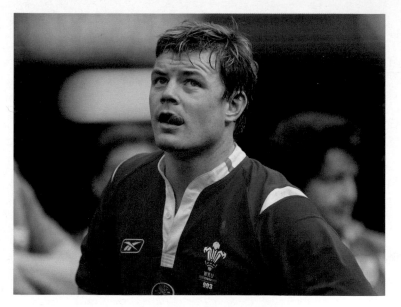

Afterwards, my face says it all.

Wearing the green in Cardiff: my sister Julie, Mum, Dad and sister Susan.

Here I wrong-foot Neil Back in our Heineken Cup quarter-final
against Leicester, but Leicester were the better team.

At Heathrow airport with Clive Woodward on the day I was named
Lions captain (*above*), and preparing to face the media (*below*).

Facing up to a Maori elder (*above*)
and accepting the first of many hakas (*below*), at Rotorua.

There are no snakes in Ireland, but there are plenty of Lions: posing with Eddie
O'Sullivan and the Irish players who were on the first plane to New Zealand.
Simon Easterby later joined us and made a big impact.

Full-dress Lions photoshoot – for some reason, Bill Beaumont
and Clive Woodward don't seem quite as amused as I do.

They start them young in New Zealand: signing autographs at North Harbour (*above*) and baby-sitting a tiny All Black (*below*).

We played some of our best rugby of the tour in the opening minutes of the opening match, against Bay of Plenty. Lawrence Dallaglio's injury midway through the first half was a huge blow.

Clive has just released the news that Jason Robinson is going to miss the first two weeks of the tour to spend some time with his pregnant wife, who is expecting in August. Jason is a big family man and normally travels on tour with his wife and three children. He is anxious about the situation and will feel a whole load better for some time at home. He is like Neil Back in that he is such a consummate professional that he will be absolutely right physically when he does fly down. It's not ideal, though, and the benefits of Clive's huge forty-five-man squad are beginning to become apparent now. Already we are travelling without Gareth Thomas and Stephen Jones, who cannot secure their release from French League commitments for another couple of weeks. Neil Back is out for his month's suspension and Michael Owen has been given permission to fly back next week to attend the birth of his child. And now Jason. It's a logistical challenge to say the least, but Louise Ramsey, Clive's operations manager, is on top of the job.

Wednesday 25 May, British Airways Lounge, Heathrow

Will soon be up in the clouds again heading for Auckland on BA 15 out of Heathrow. The tour has officially started, and I couldn't be happier. Gavin Henson has dyed his hair red for the occasion and makes quite a sight getting a coffee over there. His girlfriend Charlotte Church is hoping to travel down for the Tests, as is Geordan's girlfriend Lucie. The rugby is going to be close but we should definitely win the sing-song afterwards, no bother.

Busy day today. Bit of light training, big press call at lunchtime with everybody present and correct, and then coaches headed up the M4 to Heathrow. Some people hate all the travelling and dislocation – and the flight to New Zealand is the mother of all journeys at just over twenty-four hours – but I am young enough to enjoy the excitement and romance of it all. Still a bit of fall-out from Monday night at the press conference, but that's probably because the scribes have very little else to write about until our official Maori welcome at Rotorua on Sunday. In our own minds the Pumas match has gone, the lessons have been learned and our resolve hardened. We are all in our number ones for the official picture on the steps of the plane but will get changed into T-shirt and trackie bottoms once we settle down for the flight.

Bit of domestic news from Leinster. Michael Cheika has been appointed director of rugby with David Knox as specialist backs coach. An all-Australian duo. Don't know an awful lot about Michael, but David has the reputation of being a very innovative operator with the backs in the mould of Pat Howard, so I am hopeful. Leinster, and Dublin for that matter, are a world away at the moment, though. Eyes only on New Zealand.

Final checklist for the flight. Passport: yes. Boarding card: yes. Mobile phones (2): yes. iPods (2): yes. Laptop: yes. PlayStation 2 (the new version, lucky me): yes. DVD on the 1950 Lions tour: yes. Ear plugs: yes. Right, that's me. Unless I suddenly get the literary urge en route, the next time you hear from me will be in New Zealand, where I will be captaining the 2005 Lions. Still like to mutter the words to myself occasionally, makes the dream seem like a reality.

Just phoned home for a long chat with Dad. He has been fantastic since the announcement of my captaincy on 11 April. It wasn't just *my* life that changed that day! He has virtually given up the day job to concentrate on fielding all the calls that have been coming in requesting interviews, appearances and endorsements, etc. He has taken care of absolutely everything and hasn't bothered me with any problems. This works because we are family. Even a good friend acting as an agent would probably feel the need to refer back to me on the big issues, and I just don't need that at the moment. I haven't got the energy or time to concentrate on anything but the tour. I trust Dad implicitly. Anyway, I said a big heartfelt thank-you to him and we had a good natter about the tour itself.

Facing the Haka

Thursday 26 May, Singapore airport

Feeling much better after a long hot shower in the business lounge. Quick stopover here at Singapore airport en route to Sydney. The majority of the party are on this plane but there aren't enough business-class seats for everybody, so there's also a Lions crowd aboard another BA flight, to Sydney via Bangkok. The plan is that we all meet up at Sydney before the final hop over to Auckland. Managed five hours' sleep during the last half of the Singapore leg thanks to a wicked knock-out tablet the doc dispensed. Clive took his in the lounge beforehand and was beginning to nod off even as he walked up the stairs to board. Have just treated myself to some flash little speakers at the duty-free to go with my iPod. Rather pleased with myself.

Friday 27 May, Hilton Hotel, Auckland

Bill Beaumont is a hero, apparently. Well, what are managers for? It seems there was an incident on the Bangkok flight – funny in retrospect, but probably a bit scary at the time – with Gavin Scott, one of our video-analysis gurus, taking one of the knock-out tabs and falling asleep midway through his meal with a bread roll stuck in his mouth and threatening to choke him. One of the air hostesses became alarmed and went up to my cousin Gary, one of our medics, and said she thought he was ill. Gary and Bill rushed back and immediately worked out what had happened. Bill gently extracted the bread roll from Gavin's throat.

Managed another five hours' sleep on the way down to Sydney and felt surprisingly good when we eventually touched down in Auckland. About 150 fans were there to greet us, which was nice, plus one New Zealand supporter who immediately challenged us with his version of the haka. That was nice as well.

Felt a bit of a fraud on the bus when Will Greenwood asked me if we would all be sharing rooms at the hotel. With all the authority a Lions captain can muster, I said, 'Yes' – only for team manager Louise Ramsey to inform us ten minutes later, to widespread cheering, that every player would have a room of his own. Apparently the rooms are too small for two large beds to be fitted. Will looked at me and made a humorous face. I made a joke of it but am annoyed with myself. I must do my homework and get these things right. Players seem to look to you much more when you are the Lions captain than when you are simply a national captain. Here, on tour, they expect you to know the answers. I suppose I am a face they all know, whereas many of the non-coaching management are still a little new to them.

Was determined to stay awake as long as possible after landing to get the body on New Zealand time. Didn't feel tired so managed to last through to 1 a.m. no problem. Went for a stroll and a couple of quiet beers along the harbour front with some of the lads to stretch our legs and continue the 'bonding'. A New Zealand photographer followed us all the way, presumably desperate for one of us to give a female supporter a hug or a kiss when signing an autograph. He was becoming a pain, so Ray had a wee word in his ear.

Intrigued by the 'Ice Bar' close to the hotel. The temperature is set at minus five degrees and they have boots and coats at the entrance for everybody to wear. It's Spala all over again – useful to know about if anybody pulls a hamstring. There is also a bar where everybody has to sit on double beds and four-posters. Interesting.

Saturday 28 May, Hilton Hotel

Decent sleep, still going strong. Jet lag, what jet lag? Brunch with Adidas people and some of their New Zealand stars – Tana Umaga, Doug Howlett and Byron Kelleher, among others. I have done photo-shoots with Tana and we immediately picked up where we left off. Pretty sure there will be a good atmosphere between the teams off the pitch. I have been trying to think who Tana reminds me of and I have finally nailed it. Paddy Johns, the former Ireland lock. Not in terms of looks – they couldn't be more different – but personality. Charming gentleman off the pitch, complete maniac on it.

Spent some good time with Jonny today, first catch-up in a long while. My God, his life has changed. Can hardly believe what he was telling me. He's virtually a prisoner, can't go anywhere without being mobbed and hassled. Full-time security guards, the works. Apart from David Beckham he is probably the most recognizable face in England, sport or otherwise. He spends so much time indoors he has already mastered the guitar and is moving on to the piano. He mentioned in an interview a few months ago that he might take up the piano; the very next morning a company were on to his people offering him one. He hasn't got room at home for a real piano, so they sent him an electronic one. I think during the long injury breaks he has had a good ponder, and he is determined to 'get his life back' after the Lions tour is over. Within the confines of the hotel and the training pitch he is the same old Jonny. Much more of a wisecracker and giggler than the public ever see. But you can see him tense up and glaze over a bit once we step out into the public arena. Suddenly realize how lucky I am in Ireland, where generally everybody gives me a good bit of space. Hope everything works out for him.

Sunday 29 May, Hilton Hotel

Spoke too soon. Bad night's sleep last night, jet lag kicking in with a vengeance. Busy and enjoyable day, though. Started off with picking up the *Sunday Herald* and seeing Lawrie Mains – who coached the All Blacks in the 1995 World Cup, if I remember correctly – slag us off as the worst Lions party ever to visit New Zealand, etc. John Mitchell was also quoted in the same, confidently predicting that we would be smashed 3–0. Not amused and determined to make them eat their words.

Never believe any sportsman who says he doesn't read the newspapers and isn't affected by what they say. Mains hasn't even seen us train, let alone play, he has absolutely nothing to base his opinion on. He must have some sort of personal agenda, or his paper must have asked specifically for a Pom-bashing piece. Most of the guys have seen it and his comments were included in the quote of the day on our daily info sheet that is pushed under the door. We will use it to our advantage, blow it up and pin it on the board of our team room.

Writing this on the plane back from Rotorua, where we have just had the official Maori welcoming ceremony. Good fun and very interesting. Unbelievable reception at the airport – thousands rather than hundreds – and then we coached it to the ceremony, which had to be held indoors because of the rain. On the way in we were told that we had to respond to a song the Maori warriors would sing with one of our own. Panic! What could we sing and who could lead? None of our Welsh players seem to have a note in their head – how times have changed – but I remembered Matt Stevens has got a great baritone voice. I asked him if he fancied it, and he immediately said yes. He went off and learned the verses of 'Bread of Heaven' in ten minutes flat. Very impressed. Confident young guy.

It was hot and steamy inside the hall, and I was sweating up a fair bit. At one stage a Maori elder next to me, who was probably nearer eighty than seventy, leaned over and asked if I was OK. Didn't realize I looked that bad. I had to make a little speech, accepting the challenge and saying that we had come not only to play good rugby but to make friends and to enjoy everything that New Zealand had to offer. It was a touching moment, not at all naff or embarrassing. Felt a real connection with past tours and a strong sense of being in a special country where our presence was important. Matt was a star when his turn came, though the rest of us in the chorus were nothing to write home about.

After a mingle, and a few autographs, it was back to the airport in our bus. We drove straight up to the steps of our chartered plane, climbed on board and five minutes later we were off. That's the way to travel.

Monday 30 May, Hilton Hotel

Just logged on to BBC online and nearly killed myself laughing at one of the pictures. Half-naked Maori warrior in face paint and feathers, eyes ablaze, tongue hanging out and armed with spear, lays down the challenge to Lions manager Bill Beaumont, immaculate in jacket and Lions tie. And the BBC caption? 'Lions manager Bill Beaumont (right) accepts the Maori challenge.' When in doubt always best to avoid any confusion I suppose.

Amused to hear from Geordan that the column he's doing for the *Guardian* was censored by our press department before it was allowed to appear this morning. He mentioned our little stroll and discreet beer-tasting session on Friday night, but this was deemed unacceptable and his ghostwriter was phoned up at 6 a.m. New Zealand time. The reference to drinks had to be changed to 'a relaxing stroll'.

Not particularly happy with this approach. Wherever possible, honesty has to be the best policy. We were doing nothing wrong, there is no need to be evasive. Over the course of two or three hours we enjoyed two or three quiet beers to wind down after thirty hours of travelling. It is actually what the medics recommend. And here we are, in effect telling a lie, to cover up something we were perfectly entitled to do. It could have amusing consequences, though. Suspect that 'relaxing stroll' will quickly become the Tour euphemism for a beer, and most of our columnists will start using the expression.

Personally I like Alastair Campbell. He is a very clever and personable guy who loves his sport, though he wouldn't claim to know a whole lot about rugby. I enjoy his company, he's always up for a bit of craic and banter. It's just that he comes from a cautious, suspicious world in which there seems to be no trust and little common sense or fair play. Little words and phrases can be seized upon to make front-page stories and cost politicians their jobs. In such a minefield the assumption is that there has to be an element of control.

Well, for me rugby just isn't like that. There may be the occasional spats and misunderstanding, but the prevailing culture is one of honesty and tolerance with large dashes of humour. Arguments can quickly be cleared up over a pint. A little bit of gamesmanship livens up proceedings occasionally – Ireland were guilty of that against Scotland, with our deception over our hamstring injuries – but we are talking about a game here. I find being briefed about what I should be saying at the next press conference hard to handle. I might not be Einstein but I pride myself on being able to think on my feet and formulate my own views and have worked hard over the last couple of years to be informative and honest. Also, being myself is much easier than having to be careful all the time.

Just back from the Zurich golf tournament, which was wet and blustery but great fun and very relaxing. I was playing with Sean Rafferty, Mark Cueto and radio journalist Andrew Titteridge. We sneaked third place in the Texas Scramble at one under, though Clive's team – featuring mainly himself and Geordan, a serious golfer – won at a canter. The golf club laid on a spectacularly delicious spread and all in all a great time was had. A 'relaxing stroll' would finish the day off perfectly, but we have had our R and R today. It's time to start concentrating fully on our first tour match, against Bay of Plenty.

Tuesday 31 May, Hilton Hotel

Much better night's sleep. Busy day. Up to North Harbour and their stadium at Albany this morning for the first of our two open training sessions. Very light workout by us because we had a full session in private this afternoon. The open session seemed to be appreciated. I would put the crowd at about 2,000, though apparently Alastair and Co. put out a release claiming 5,000! In the great scheme of things it doesn't really matter, I suppose, but it all seems unnecessary. We did an Open Day, it was a heartfelt gesture, we enjoyed it, and a fair few people turned up. End of story. Can't see the need to embellish it.

Couple of amusing snippets. Miles Harrison from Sky TV was doing a commentary for the crowd and we had to do an official run-on. I went sprinting on and of course the rest stitched me up and stayed put in the tunnel, leaving me looking like a Billy-No-Mates as I ran around the pitch on my own. I must have been out there fifteen to twenty seconds – which seems like a very long time indeed – before anybody bothered to join me.

Then there was the Lions promotional video on the big screen, which highlighted, among others, the following well-known players: Ian O'Driscoll, Reth Cooper, TT Dawson, Vin Henson, Ane Horgan, Ordan Murphy, Nan O'Gara, Son Robinson, Il Back, Chard Hill, Thin Jenkins, Wis Moody, Mon Taylor, Dy Sheridan and his front-row mates Eve Thompson and Lian White. It seems the big screen wasn't big enough, and cut off the first two letters of everybody's Christian name. The legacy could be permanent, with Steve

Thompson and Gethin Jenkins already saddled with new nicknames.

One New Zealand supporter, with a fine sense of the ridiculous, was handing out spoof 'I Spy a Lion' cards, inviting competitors to spot all 76 members of the party before the final test on 9 July. Scores ranged from a paltry ten for my good self and Sir Clive Woodward to a whopping 500 for assistant kit technician David 'Don' Pearson and chef Dave Campbell.

With no midweek game, afternoon training was a rare opportunity for everybody to run out together. Clive and the coaches thought it was too shambolic, and they've decided on no more group sessions. Didn't think it was that bad!

Wednesday 1 June, Hilton Hotel

Clive and Eddie go through yesterday afternoon's video highlighting our many mistakes. Have to admit it was a bit sloppy. 'There's only three words to describe it,' declared Eddie solemnly: 'Un ac cept able.' I make that four syllables rather than three words, but he got a laugh anyway, and the tension eased a bit. It was a good honest session and we went out and put in our best training session of the tour to date this afternoon, everybody working with a will.

Had another chat with Alastair this afternoon. There is no doubt he is good company. Told me a nice story about Prince William, who will be our guest for the final two weeks of the tour, visiting the England changing room after the 2002 football World Cup match against Argentina. Michael Owen hadn't noticed the Prince had slipped into the room and was walking around as naked as the day he was born when presented to HRH. Neither apparently batted an eyelid. He will have to get used to that down here with us, but I am told he is a keen rugby player and knows the score.

Thursday 2 June, Hilton Hotel

Day off ahead of the match. Just had James Robson, the tour's head doctor, on the phone to say that Malcolm O'Kelly will have to fly home: his injury hasn't settled and there is no realistic chance of him playing on tour. The medics, who have been superb, sorted out the abdominal muscle tear but in so doing unearthed a groin problem that has been niggling Malcolm on and off for a while. And at the moment it's definitely on rather than off. Mal is still up in town somewhere, coming back from the specialists, so I haven't been able to have a word. Feel for him. He wanted to put the record straight after enjoying a less than happy tour in 2001. He has been in great form this season and would have challenged hard for a Test spot. Mentally he was absolutely right for this tour and now the moment has gone. Just reinforces what I have always felt, namely that you have to take every opportunity that comes your way in life. You never know what calamity is just around the corner.

Been mooching around in my room catching up on sleep, phoning home, reading a book. Nipped over to the casino for a quick go on the pokies and a look at what games they have on the tables. Caribbean Stud Poker is my favourite and it's there all right. About time I got my eye back in. Went for a wander and circled the Sky Tower. Am tempted to have a go at the bungee jump. I'm not usually an adventure sports freak but am tempted just to see if I've got the bottle. Not today, but perhaps later in the tour.

Crazy golf challenge with Richard Hill in the team room this afternoon, followed by table tennis. Honours even. All very relaxed. Calm before the storm again, I suppose. Feeling good though, very composed. Not too anxious and impatient like I can be. Very controlled.

Was chatting to James Robson, who is another of nature's gentlemen. He did a session with the press this morning when he indicated pretty clearly that Malcolm was struggling and that there could be developments tonight. James tells things as they are and rocked the media back a little when he said he had treated thirty-eight of the forty-five players since the tour began. You could misconstrue that and go away with the impression that we are a bunch of hypochondriacs or extremely unhealthy. In reality we are just athletes who have to look after our bodies. Most the time we just check in with James with simple things like a headache or upset stomach just to make sure it's nothing serious. And you have to be so careful taking any over-the-counter medicines these days – almost everything seems to be on the banned list – so again James will be our first port of call there. I'm not sure his honesty with the press in these matters was welcomed in some quarters, but facts are facts. We are a large travelling group 12,000 miles away from home, and the squad doctor is always going to be a busy man.

Had a quick catch-up with Danny Grewcock, with whom I roomed in Australia in 2001. He is such a nice guy away from rugby, and such a brute of a second-row on the pitch. Glad he's on our side. We need tough guys like Danny putting their bodies on the line.

The boys for the Taranaki game came in from their day

off full of the joys. A crew led by Lewis Moody were off on a turkey shoot and returned with sixteen or seventeen birds. They asked the hotel chef to cook them, which they did, and it looked delicious, but Lewis has just nearly choked on a large lump of shot. Tried very hard not to laugh.

Friday 3 June, Rotorua

Chilling out in my hotel room reading Dan Brown's *Angels and Demons*. Really hooked, can't put it down, just like *The Da Vinci Code*. Very therapeutic, because we are just twenty-four hours away now from the opening game in New Zealand against Bay of Plenty, and I can feel the nerves bubbling away underneath. Very smooth day so far. Trained this morning in Auckland, flew down to Rotorua at lunch-time, had a walk-through at the stadium and then back to the hotel for a couple of final meetings. Everybody pulling together nicely.

Lawrence has been a tower of strength this week. He is so up for this game and has got the forwards buzzing around him. He was awesome in training on Wednesday, and has done a lot of the press this week, which has taken the pressure off me. He looks mean, moody and magnificent at the moment, and even the Kiwis have been impressed with his approach. He is a leader by nature – and there is no doubt that he would have dreamed about captaining the Lions him-self one day – but I couldn't ask for a better and more loyal number two. He has given me his total support from day one. It's funny – we Celts often talk about our passion and patriotism and suppose that England are all power and method, but I have never met two more heart-on-the-sleeve rugby players than Martin Johnson and Lawrence Dallaglio. They have been the soul of English rugby for a decade now. It has been very reassuring to have Lawrence by my side this week.

So here we go. How many people in the world ever have a dream come true? I am a lucky man and will try and enjoy every last second of tomorrow's match. Must phone Mum and Dad and Glenda in a few hours for one final chat before the game. I like to turn my phone off first thing on match day and ignore it until after the game. Just hope we can get off to a decent start tomorrow. A win first up is everything.

Saturday 4 June, Rotorua

Lawrence is in hospital with a broken ankle. Really nasty injury. Just shattered by the news, he is such a big player for us and has been such a fantastic ally for me on this tour. He seems so indestructible, it never occurred to me that he would get injured. When we got back to the changing room about an hour ago I turned on the mobile phone for the first time and the first message waiting for me was a text Lawrence had sent me this morning. 'Just wanted you to know my friend how proud I will be running out behind you tonight. You will lead the Lions like the true champion you are. Good luck, Lol.' And now he's on the hospital bed, off the tour and wondering if his career is over. Started filling up with the emotion of the day and had to find a quiet corner for a few seconds to compose myself. This can be a bloody cruel game sometimes. Am just scribbling this in my notepad on the way to the official reception. I am full of thoughts and memories and snapped mental images of the day at the moment and need to sit down properly tomorrow to try and make sense of it all. Mum has been on and even she – a confirmed non-blubber, at least in public – admitted to a few tears 12,000 miles back in Dublin as she watched her lad run on with the stuffed Lion held aloft. What a day.

Sunday 5 June, Hilton Hotel, Auckland

Lazy Sunday afternoon. I've got no mind to worry! So much to say and now, finally, time to marshal my thoughts and say it. Just back from Rotorua and I have got a long afternoon stretching ahead of me with absolutely nothing planned except a few coffees and scribbling these notes. Can't think of anything better. Am really enjoying writing this diary, it makes me step back a little and think that little bit harder about what has been going on. Captaining the Lions in New Zealand – just a handful of rugby players have ever had that honour and I want to absorb every moment.

Firstly the match.

We got worked up at the hotel just before leaving. Gareth Jenkins, one of our assistant coaches, presented the Lions shirts individually and made each of us feel ten feet tall. Gareth, who coaches at Llanelli, is a passionate West Walian rugby nut who just missed out on Lions selection in the late seventies and early eighties. He trained under Carwyn James at Llanelli and provides a tenuous link with the famous '71 squad, which is revered down here. He would have given his right arm to have played for the Lions just once, in fact he still would. He was absolutely the perfect man for the occasion, although funnily enough he only stepped in at the last moment when Ian McGeechan – the Lions head coach on no fewer than three occasions – got stranded after attending a ceremony somewhere. There was a hitch with the helicopter and he was running late, so Clive asked Gareth to step in. Inspired decision. Gareth was nearly in tears when he solemnly handed over the shirts and told us with the great honour came responsibility. We must not just look like Lions, we had to play like Lions. We must not just pay lip service to the traditions, we must aim to make history ourselves. He has a magnificent way of saying the word 'passion' – he turns it into a sentence rather than a word. 'Paaaashuuuun'. I often seem to be mumbling 'paaaashuuuun' to myself these days. I could listen to him talk all day. Anyway, by the time Gareth had finished we were pretty pumped up, I can tell you.

With our police escort from the hotel we arrived at 5.30 p.m., a full hour and forty minutes before the start. Apparently it's an England thing, they like to get to the ground early enough for Jonny to go through his kicking drills, but that's much too soon for my liking. I like to arrive, get changed, do my own stretch for about ten minutes, go through the team warm-up for half an hour and then back into the dressing room for ten minutes before showtime. From the moment of arrival I like a sharp and steady build-up to the kick-off, no faffing about killing time. Bang, bang, bang. Arrive, warm up, play.

Have just talked to Clive about it, and he has put his hands up straight away and admitted it was a cock-up and that we will make everything much tighter for the rest of the tour. It's not a huge issue, but we pride ourselves on our attention to detail and I wasn't the only one a bit twitchy at having my normal routine changed. We are all creatures of habit and like everything just right, especially when we are stressed.

The match was a fabulous occasion under the lights at

Rotorua International Stadium. Great crowd – 35,000, they
reckon – and very atmospheric with the Maori dancers doing
their stuff before kick-off. It was all very theatrical: the stadium is a natural amphitheatre with many of the people sitting
or standing on the huge grass banks. Good job it wasn't
raining.

Prolonged build-up or not, we were out of the blocks like
a rocket and played fifteen minutes of faultless rugby – I can't
remember a single handling error. Josh Lewsey powered over
for two tries after superb continuity work by forwards and
backs, and then Ronan O'Gara put in one of his cross-field
kicks and Mark Cueto, as cool as you like on these occasions,
dobbed it down: 17–0, and we were absolutely flying. It all
seemed remarkably easy. One more score then and we probably would have been away and out of sight, but Bay of
Plenty are a cracking little side – third in the NPC last year
– and, lifted by the crowd and their own pride, they began
to bring their very useful running backs into play.

They had pulled one try back through their number 8 and
we were trying to batten down the hatches for ten minutes
when disaster struck for Lawrence. I remember very little of
the actual incident except that we were both trying to stop
the same man. I watched the video half an hour ago, and you
can see that his studs catch a bit as we all fall awkwardly. I
heard him scream out in pain straight away and saw James
Robson sprint on as play continued – BOP were in a good
position and pressing for a second try. We held them off and
finally the ref could stop play. James managed to get the
dislocated ankle put back in, and I think he gave Lawrence
something for the pain as they lifted him on to the golf cart.
He got a fantastic ovation from everybody as he went off, a
real warrior leaving the arena. Most of the fans probably

thought it was the last time they would see Lawrence involved in international rugby, but I wouldn't be so sure. No matter how serious the injury, Lawrence will be determined to return because that's the way he is.

We were disrupted and upset by everything, it is pointless to deny that, so we simply had to weather the storm and survive until half-time. The second quarter was bloody hard work as BOP threw everything at us. They got another try and a penalty to make it 17–17 at half-time, but I felt confident and in control as we went down the tunnel.

'Right, we start again; it's 0–0 and we take it from here. Let's get some possession, keep the ball or kick deep into their corners. They want to hit us with everything but will get frustrated if we keep pinning them back.' Clive and Eddie said much the same and that's exactly what we did. We also put on fresh kit, as we will be doing at every match. The second half is another game and we must go again. Putting on new jerseys and shorts just helps reinforce that.

ROG, who had been struggling with his goal-kicking, didn't miss a beat as he played the corners game, which he is well used to doing with Munster. Gradually we built momentum and then the tries started coming again: Tom Shanklin, Dwayne Peel and finally Gordon D'Arcy, courtesy of a cracking break from Josh off a set move we have been working on. It should have been four, but after my one real break of the night I managed to mess things up. I had an unmarked Mark Cueto calling for the ball on the outside and Josh steaming up on the inside. I chose Josh when it should have gone out wide. Adrian Cashmore did well in defence, but I was annoyed with myself and deserved the bollocking Mark began to give me. Then he suddenly realized he was slagging off the captain and started apologizing! No worries, it was bad play from me and I was as annoyed as Mark. He should have heard the language I was using!

Mixed emotions at the final whistle: 34–20. Excitement at what I thought was an exceptional game of rugby and occasion, one of the best I have been part of. Pleasure at a job well done in the second half when I felt we grew as a team, annoyance at going off the boil in the second quarter and finally a little bit of despair at losing Lawrence so early in the tour.

We headed for the tunnel to clap BOP off, but they were doing a well-deserved lap of honour, so we waited four or five minutes for them to finish their celebrations. All the New Zealand media this morning mentioned what a nice gesture that was, but sure it was only good manners. They had been great opponents and we wanted to see them off properly. There was an excellent spirit throughout the game and we had shared a special rugby occasion. It's easy to see why Lions matches live in the memories of those who watch them. I did a lengthy TV interview afterwards and was surprised how poised and together I felt.

It turned into a late night but not a boisterous one. There was no point even thinking about sleep, I was so pumped up and buzzing, but I didn't much fancy a big night either. These are very early days, and Lawrence's injury had taken the gloss off things for me. Ended up down the Pig and Whistle in town and enjoyed a few songs with the lads in the corner as I sipped my way quietly through a couple of beers. Finally got to have a few words with Malcolm O'Kelly. He is very philosophical. He wanted this tour badly but there is much more in Malcolm's life than just rugby. He is one of those characters who will definitely get over the disappointment and move on. Ended up walking back to the hotel for a cuppa in the lobby about 3 a.m., a weird experience with all the steam from the geysers that Rotorua is famous for. Loads of people still around. Can't believe there are so many Lions supporters over so early.

Have got the TV on in the corner. Watching Norman Hewitt, the former All Black hooker, cover himself in glory in *Dancing with the Stars*, the NZ version of *Strictly Come Dancing*. He is absolutely brilliant. Sensational. He and his partner have just got four straight tens from the judges for his pasa doble, with a haka thrown in in the middle for fun. He is easily the best competitor and has to win the whole programme if there is any justice. What is it about hookers? Lots of them seem to be mad extroverts. Hewitt, Keith Wood, Brian Moore, to name just three. Blood brothers obviously.

Lawrence has just arrived back at the hotel after his operation, so it's time to find the big man to welcome him back. James says he won't be able to travel for ten days or a fortnight, so he will be around the place. Hopefully I can catch up with him and then I might just nip out for a 'relaxing stroll'. The tour is moving on quickly. Simon Shaw has arrived already as Malcolm's replacement in the squad, having flown straight from London where he was getting ready to play in the Martin Johnson testimonial game. He looks fit and ready for the fray. I remember reading somewhere that Simon got called into England's 2003 World Cup squad but never played and gave his winner's medal to a friend. I can understand that.

Monday 6 June, Hilton Hotel

Went into the gym expecting a light rehab workout on my legs – the old war wound on my left shoulder is playing up again, so I am trying to rest that completely – and Dave Reddin hits us with a monster session. I was sweating buckets by the end and nearly collapsed. But it was exhilarating. I don't know if it is just the freshness that a new face like Dave brings to the training, or his different techniques, or just the fact that I am so motivated, but I am achieving levels of fitness I never contemplated before.

Then this afternoon the squad for Saturday's game against New Zealand Maori put in a quality team session – very little contact work, but loads of passing and interplay before forwards and backs went over some patterns together. Generally speaking, looked good. We went as hard as we felt we wanted to: we are not into unnecessary beasting on this trip. Drove down to training in the coach accompanied by Tom Shanklin's Power Ballad tape – *Top Gun* music, Madonna's 'Holiday', 'Lady in Red' – all those tunes you don't really think you know or like but can't help singing along to. Happy music to put a smile on our faces.

With Lawrence injured and his replacement Simon Easterby en route, Martin Corry has been pressed into service for his third consecutive game, against Taranaki, having started instead of the injured Simon Taylor against the Pumas and then replaced Lawrence midway through the first half on Saturday night. This time he will be captaining from number 8, and I know he is as proud as punch. By midweek the Lions 2005 should be at full strength. Stephen Jones got in from France last Friday, Simon Shaw arrived last night, Gareth

Thomas is on his way after Toulouse got knocked out of the French championship at the semi-final stage, and Jason Robinson has left Heathrow.

After initially wondering quite how such a big squad would work, I am a total convert. The idea is to produce a fit, healthy and specifically prepared squad of twenty-two for every match on tour, which should in turn lead to the best-prepared Test-match line-up we can hope to produce. To do that we need a minimum of forty-four players. The Kiwis still seem obsessed by the size of our party, but, having seen how it works in practice, I could make a strong case for fifty or more players. And if you have that number of players to train, prepare, cater for and generally pamper, then you need the Jumbo-sized non-playing squad Clive has assembled.

The reaction of the New Zealand public and media is pleasantly positive . . . so far. They all seem delighted that it was such a successful occasion at Rotorua on Saturday – with their bid for the 2011 World Cup under the microscope they are determined that every match day goes off without a hitch – and the bottom line is that it was a cracking game of rugby, full of tries and incident. My impression is that they are going to give us the benefit of the doubt in the early weeks, but I am under no illusions: come the Tests, we will have all sorts thrown at us.

Just back from a relaxing meal down on Auckland harbour front. Scallops and lots of them – they're my favourite seafood, and I eat them a lot at home. There was a funny moment when this distinguished-looking lady came up with a mobile phone and asked if Clive could talk to her nephew, I think it was, who was celebrating his birthday. Clive went into his best patter, thinking it was a kid.

'Hello, it's Clive Woodward here with the Lions squad in

Auckland. I understand it's your birthday. And how old are you today?'

'Thirty-five,' came the answer.

'Thirty-five!' shouted Clive in utter disbelief, but he could see the rest of us cracking up and started laughing himself. My sympathies are with him. I absolutely hate being asked to talk to absolute strangers on the phone like that. Just can't do it.

About a dozen of us were crowded around the table with Clive, a good lively mix. Chris Cusiter was there with his girlfriend, a gorgeous lass, who is over for a week or so, and it was funny watching all of us manoeuvre at the table trying to get within speaking distance of her. Female company is in pretty short supply at the moment and just ten minutes shooting the breeze with her about anything at all – except rugby – was very much appreciated.

I phone Glenda just about every night, which is fantastic and makes sure I end every day on a high. I also have a 'girl-pal' – I think that's the right expression these days for a female friend who you are not dating – who sends me very amusing emails which make me laugh out loud and keep the spirits up. She knows the rugby scene well enough but sees everything from a woman's perspective and hammers the nail on the head when we mere males are being ridiculous or getting everything out of all proportion. Jules and Sue email me two or three times a week and keep me up to date with all the Dublin gossip. Rugby is such a male-dominated environment, especially on tour, that it's important to keep close to the women in your life!

Mum has taken over control of the computer back in Clontarf and sends a little message of support every day. I phone the folks regularly, of course, but the time difference can make it really difficult. When they are up and about, you are tired and ready for your bed and vice versa.

Just back from the casino after another little session of Caribbean Stud poker. Down at present but feel my luck is about to change.

Tuesday 7 June, in bed, Hilton Hotel

Woke up feeling sick and my shoulder was humming a bit as well. And it was all going so well! Tried to battle on at training but eventually had to come back to the hotel, where I was violently sick. The doc says it is food poisoning from the scallops and didn't I know better than to eat them abroad in match week? Really don't feel well at all. Propped up here in bed sweating and with a headache, trying to read but just snoozing really and listening to my iPod. Darce has just popped in to sympathize, if that is the right word. For some reason he finds it highly amusing. Suppose that's what friends are for.

Wednesday 8 June, New Plymouth, then Auckland

I'm through the worst of the food poisoning but still feeling a bit delicate. Have lost 3 or 4 kg in the last twenty-four hours. But the show must always go on. It's a matter of mind over matter, and I had a busy day to get through. Firstly those of us not playing against Taranaki ironed out a few kinks in another light session and then flew up to New Plymouth for one of our community days — and what an eye-opener that was. The schoolboys were about sixteen — huge lads — and what I oversaw was a full-on contact session. They boshed the living daylights out of each other for over an hour. I couldn't train like that every day. In one way it was deeply impressive, but I was also left wondering how they ever learned the basic ball skills. As I was still a bit crook I wasn't kitted out for training – I was in blazer and Lions anorak – but I couldn't resist the temptation to start spinning out a few passes with some of the lads on the touchline, just to make the point! One of the mums was there with a new-born baby and she asked me to do a little baby-sitting while she concentrated on the training. Happy to oblige. She was a gorgeous wee thing dressed in her little All Blacks shirt. She was good as gold sitting on my lap, and we seemed to get on just fine. Shane Williams came up to me and pointed to one of the lads, who had long hair, dishing out the bosh, and said:

'Who does that remind you of?'

'Don't know.'

'Sonia from *Eastenders*.'

He bloody well did as well. They say that everybody has their double somewhere in the world.

Talking of look-alikes. Stacks of New Zealanders, mostly girls, seem to think Josh Lewsey is Jonny Wilkinson. It's really getting to him now, and of course we don't wind him up at all.

Driving around, I got a very good vibe about New Plymouth and Taranaki in general. It was a spectacular bright morning. On one side you see the 6,000ft Mount Egmont, a snow-covered volcano, and on the other were some of New Zealand's top surf beaches. A spectacular spot in the summer, I would say. The mountain was used as the backdrop for the Tom Cruise film *The Last Sumarai*, and apparently Cruise was keen on buying some property here. Can understand why.

Drove past a fantastic-looking golf course on the way back, would have loved to hop out and hit a few balls, but it wouldn't do my shoulder much good. It seems a very buzzy place, and for a while I was puzzled why I could hear so many American accents, until our driver told us that New Plymouth is the servicing port for some off-shore oil rigs out in the Tasman Sea. Where there is oil there are generally Americans.

From training and a quick snoop about New Plymouth it was back to the hotel for some food and the presentation of the jerseys before the match. It's important the entire squad is together for this occasion so that those selected know that they are representing us all and that they have our total support. When you are out there putting your body on the line it is us – the group of people you find yourself with – that you fight for first, and then comes the Lions jersey and the tradition that goes with it. Ian McGeechan make a short but powerful speech. What a contribution to the Lions he has made. Two tours as a player, three as a coach, including the successful trips to Australia in 1989 and South Africa in 1997, and now this, his sixth tour. He has our total respect, and the players listen closely to what he has to say. After that it was off down to the Yarrow Stadium, and yet again we managed to get to the stadium too early. Our drivers know all the back routes and the traffic never seems as bad as the police and locals predict.

The match was another cracker and again we finished very strongly in the second half to complete a highly satisfactory win. Taranaki were probably a bit stronger up front than BOP, but didn't quite have the destructive runners we encountered last Saturday. For forty minutes it was very tough going indeed and there was stacks of defending to do before we got on top after the break. Felt we got a bad decision midway through the half when Shane Horgan caught a beautiful cross-field kick from Charlie Hodgson and fed Geordan Murphy for what would have been the try of the tour to date, but Steve Walsh on the touchline, some way distant from the play, called it as a forward pass. A poor call and one which slowed our momentum as we were trying to establish ourselves in the first half. A couple of minutes later he called a knock-on by Lewis Moody from a restart after it had clearly gone off Lewis's head. Too many of these little fifty–fifties are going against us at present.

The atmosphere was superb and there was a little bonus at the game when I met up with my cousin Jenny, who is going out with Donncha O'Callaghan. Jenny and Donncha's mum are touring around all of New Zealand for the entire tour together in a little camper van. 'It will make or break them,' joked Donncha. It was great to see Jenny's friendly face and catch up with the family gossip.

Thought the boys played very well, ground out the result after a hard, physical first half when they fully tested us. Our fitness and class told in the end. Geordan finished his two tries very well and showed that magical touch of his to put Shane in for his. A good reply to Josh's top game at BOP. That's how it has to work on a successful tour, everybody pushing each other hard. Charlie Hodgson was another to have a very good game: he controlled things beautifully at 10 and you could see his confidence growing. He's got all the skills and kicked his goals well. Martin Corry scored the other try, just getting the decision from the TMO. It was a close call and we couldn't have complained if it had gone against us.

After the game it was straight back to Auckland for those of us playing New Zealand Maori, and here I am back in my room writing the day up.

Thursday 9 June, Hilton Hotel

Finally completely human again. Day off, so a chance to take stock after a busy period. Clive lets us do anything we want on our day off, and that includes spending time with your partner or wife if they are over and even having a glass of wine with your meal if you choose to dine out. 'Relaxing strolls' are far from frowned upon within the squad. Clive trusts you totally to behave in an adult and appropriate manner. The vast majority of us, contrary to public expectation, would be very wary of drinking just forty-eight hours before a big match, but if somebody does want a glass of red with their meal tonight, nobody will bat an eyelid. Put my civvies and shades on and enjoyed a good stomp around town. Once the morning fog cleared it was a gorgeous day, bright and crisp. Nipped into the casino again and, as I predicted, my luck began to change. Now I am showing a modest little profit. Took myself off for a haircut as well along with Shaggy. There were no paparazzi waiting for us, unlike when Gavin Henson went for a trim to what one of the Sunday papers here called his 'designer hedgehog'. Of course the woman cutting away at my hair used to work in Dublin and knows all my favourite hang-outs.

A couple of fans wander up and politely ask for autographs, which is no bother at all. A few of them want shirts signed, which again is not a problem. The only thing that ever really narks me with fans is if they ask me to sign something for charity or for a club fundraiser and then disappear only to turn up with three of four other items for me to sign as well. That makes me feel used and exploited.

Back for a massage followed by a read and a few calls home.

The nerves are beginning to build already and the match is still forty-eight hours away. It has been billed as the fourth Test, and I have no doubts it will be played in a Test-match atmosphere. The Maori are a proud race and their squad is packed with All Blacks. I read in the *New Zealand Herald* this morning that something like 35 per cent of all professional rugby players in New Zealand are eligible to represent New Zealand Maori. There is very little doubt that if they competed as a separate nation they would be well capable of reaching the quarter-finals of the World Cup, or maybe even better. This is a bloody serious game early in the tour.

Poor Simon Taylor is off a Lions tour for the second time with injury – his hamstring has failed to come good in time. Disappointed for him. Have come to appreciate his dry humour, and with Lawrence out of contention he was definitely a contender for the Test team.

Have just been watching the *Rugby Magazine* programme on TV1, which brings a smile. It's about as sophisticated as RTE back in the eighties, but the action is good. The presenter, Melodie Robinson, has six studio guests, which is about four too many, but I am very pleased to hear one of them, former All Black wing Stu Wilson, refuse to join in the general slagging-off of the Lions. He said he had been impressed by what he has seen to date, we would gather momentum as the tour progressed, and if we sneaked the first Test it would all get very interesting indeed. Which concurs exactly with my own views.

I then watched the weather forecast on TV1. Their expert – one Brendan Horan – said the weather tomorrow was going to be 'bloody ugly, just like the Lions front row'. Has he seen the All Black guys?!

Friday 10 June, Hamilton

The old routine. Light training in the morning, down to the hotel in Hamilton and meetings before the game tomorrow. The mood is excited but pretty apprehensive. Outside of Test rugby, games don't come much bigger than this.

I spent half an hour this evening doing a little research on the internet. Just type 'Maori Rugby' into Yahoo and suddenly you have the choice of about 10,000 entries to read. I made do with the first two.

The eligibility process governing those who can play for New Zealand Maori is very complicated. Those wishing to be considered have their credentials examined by the Maori kaumatua, or cultural advisor, who will trace the players' whakapapa, or genealogy. Apparently one year Christian Cullen scraped in by the skin of his teeth, being deemed 1/64th Maori! I would say they would be keen enough to make the connection there.

Though the Maoris gave the haka to the All Blacks team, they will not be performing the standard 'Ka Mate' before tomorrow night's game. Instead they will be chanting the 'Timatanga', which tells the story of a gathering of young warriors and chiefs declaring their ambition and desire for knowledge, unity and excellence. Sounds a bit like the Lions to me.

There was a nice paragraph from our friend Norm Hewitt, Mr Twinkle-toes, which I might contribute to our quote-of-the-day section: 'Your body does things that it has never done before, not even with the ABs. You run faster, get to the breakdown quicker, hit rucks harder. You find yourself in odd positions and you can feel ever so slightly out of control, which is why we can be brilliant one moment and not so great the next, though we tightened things up a little bit in the modern era.'

I was also amazed to read about the origins of Maori rugby and the 107-match world tour undertaken by the New Zealand Natives in 1888 and 1889. After an internal tour of New Zealand they called off for two matches in Melbourne and played an extraordinary seventy-four in Britain. Then they sailed back to Australia for a twenty-four-match tour and finished off with another eight games in New Zealand. Fourteen months away from home and 107 matches, of which they won seventy-eight. And we think seven weeks away from home is a drag!

Caught a little bit of the highlights of New Zealand v Fiji up in North Harbour this evening. 91–0 to the Blacks with fifteen tries. They looked exceptionally slick behind the scrum, but to be honest some of the tackling looked very optional. Graham Henry and his crew probably wouldn't be that happy with the game as a final workout before the first Test. They haven't played together since November – when they admittedly thrashed the French – and the kind of opposition they encountered against Fiji was not great. They sailed through the early stages of the last World Cup and looked a million dollars, as they always do against lesser opposition, but as soon as they came up against serious opposition – Australia in the semi-final – they failed to perform. Have to say though their latest Fijian – Sitiveni Sivivatu – looks some player. He strolled in for four tries and no wonder he had taken over from his cousin Joe Rokocoko. Big Joe has got serious wheels, but the new guy looks tricky as well. Fully expect him to be lining up against us in the first Test.

Gordon D'Arcy has gone down with food poisoning after a monster scallop session in Auckland last night. Karma. I am resisting the temptation to smirk.

Saturday 11 June, Hamilton

Beaten 19–13, the first Lions side ever to lose to the Maori. Very disappointed and down. They were terrific and very physical, especially at the breakdown, but none of us played well. Mystified. We trained well and seemed very up for it. Lawrence handed out the shirts before the game and gave one of his great rabble-rousing speeches. The old goosebumps were going. He would have been a huge help to me on the field. There's not much doubt in my mind that if he had not chosen to retire from international rugby last year he could have been appointed the 2005 Lions captain.

Everything seemed set fair for a big performance, but we fell flat. It wasn't for the lack of trying – in fact we tackled superbly – but something was missing. Scribbling these notes before the official function. There seems to be a bit of a delay. Very subdued Lions party.

Furious with Steve Walsh's refereeing, he was very poor and simply not up to scratch at this level. He also treats me like a school-kid. As captain I am fully entitled to seek an explanation for a decision or to bring something to his attention, but he refused to listen to me. He waved me away like an eight-year-old at a mini-rugby session. It is an insult to the Lions shirt as much as to me. He was so arrogant. Some of his decisions defied any sort of analysis. He was penalizing us at the breakdown, yet the Maori were getting away with exactly the same offences all the time. At one point I said if he was not willing to referee that part of the game we might have to take things into our own hands. 'See what happens if you do,' he snapped at me. He missed the Maori backs running all kinds of illegal blocker line. It was such a fast game that after some passages of play I wanted to say something but just didn't have the breath left. It was quite comical in that sense.

You would almost think Walsh was the star of the show and the reason there was a sell-out crowd of 30,000 fans at the Waikato Stadium tonight. Not so. We are all seething about him but we daren't say anything in public or else the New Zealand media will be on our backs and we will be labelled 'whinging poms'. Plus, Walsh is going to be involved in all our games outside of the internationals. There is actually a massive issue here. I have been refereed by all these Kiwi guys in internationals in the northern hemisphere or the World Cup, and their interpretation of the laws down here in New Zealand is completely different. They simply are not the same officials, they show no consistency, which makes it very difficult to play the game how they want it played.

I just about managed to choke back my complaints during the live TV interview afterwards and had composed myself a little for the press conference, though I was still very angry at our poor showing. Big Paul O'Connell came in with me and tried to explain what a mess the breakdown situation had become. 'Perhaps we stood off a little too much, but that's the last time it will happen on this tour,' he said in that smiling but threatening way of his. Good man, Paul, we need you to take over the Lawrence role.

Despite our two specific complaints – Steve Walsh generally and the breakdown situation specifically – we can have no arguments about actually losing. Maori were supercharged and Marty Holah and Jonno Gibbs immense up front, real warriors both of them. Fantastic players. Funnily enough, we could have still won at the death when Martyn Williams made a great break and Josh Lewsey was held back by Piri Weepu when he was steaming up to take the scoring pass. A Lions victory would have been ill-deserved, though, and might have masked aspects of our game that needed to be worked on. We can't play that badly again and expect to defeat teams like the Maori, let alone the ABs.

Ian McGeechan was very good back in the changing room. He just called for two minutes' hush and spelt out a very simple message. Defeats like this can make a Lions tour, in fact they can be a huge stepping stone. The example he used was in 1997 when the Lions Saturday 'Test' team were turned over by a modestly rated Northern Transvaal side at Pretoria just two weeks before the first Test. The Lions had been out-gunned up front and save for a few moments of brilliance from Jeremy Guscott nothing much had gone right behind the scrum.

'For about half an hour we were down, but then the true nature of the Lions squad came through,' said Geech. 'We decided there and then there would be no excuses, we would do whatever needed doing to fix the scrums, there would be no bickering and recriminations, and we would just go out there and blitz every South African team that came our way. Four days later John Bentley scored the try of his life against Gauteng and the tour was up and running again.'

Good words, which I am latching on to. Phil Larder was also excellent and praised our defence, rightly. Clive's line was, 'This will make us rather than break us.' That's what we have to do: concentrate on the good, work on the bad. I just told the lads to ignore the crap that will be written about us over the next forty-eight hours. We will be written off and rubbished. We know it is coming and it doesn't matter, as long as we truly believe we are a good team who will get better. Which we will. Better finish here. Time to accept another haka or two and make a little speech. Would I be offending anybody if I said you can only have so much of the haka in any one day? I'm nearly word-perfect now, I almost chant it along with them.

Sunday 12 June, Crown Plaza Hotel, Christchurch

As soon as I got a chance to speak to Clive after the match last night I made it quite clear I wanted play against Wellington this Wednesday. We have got to get back on the horse immediately. He seemed pretty happy with that but wanted to run it past some of the senior management, and I suspect he was also wondering about changing a couple of other planned selections. Anyway, in my mind I had already decided I was doubling up and decided to keep away from the beers and get back to the hotel ASAP after the formalities. No chance of much sleep with my mind racing and replaying a really poor performance, but at least I could rest up. Clive soon came back with the selection for Wellington and it's a very strong team. Jason Robinson and Gareth Thomas, as was always planned, make their tour debuts, and Jonny plays his first Lions game in NZ in what could conceivably be the Test back division. Up front Neil Back returns after his suspension. Shane Byrne gets a chance to press his Test claims in the front row packing alongside Julian White and Gethin Jenkins. Simon Easterby gets a start at blindside. Interesting one. Simon is a special player when the force is with him. He loves hard, physical games and Wellington might be just that.

Not happy with my own performance on Saturday. I fell off a couple of tackles and didn't kick well. I was happy enough with the second-half try, though, picked out a nice cutback line early on, was going to look to pass to Shane Williams as planned, but the gap opened up and nothing was going to stop me. As the dust settles I am also encouraged by our defence. That was a classy Maori back division, and apart from when Leon MacDonald wriggled through a few tackles – mine included – to score, they didn't really threaten. We did a great job snuffing them out. You can't win matches from your own half, though, and we have got to win more ball and control it better if we are going to prosper on this tour.

The post-match reception was quite fun. The Maori guys got the guitars out and started the singing. I contemplated stitching ROG up and saying he would reply on our behalf by singing 'Lady in Red' but decided to play it straight. The lads still weren't in the best of humour, so I just congratulated the Maori team on a wonderful win and the organizers for staging another cracking night's rugby.

Had some food about 2 a.m. back at the hotel, made a few calls home and collapsed in my bed. Was up early this morning for a rehab session in the pool, iced baths, Jacuzzi, the works. Have got a bit of a dead leg and my shoulder is bloody sore but I am not even going to countenance the possibility of being injured this week. It seemed to ease in the pool anyway. This is a must-play match. After a light lunch it was straight into the best session of the tour so far. Everybody appreciated the importance of Wednesday and we went up two or three notches this morning. Quite fiery up front and generally there was a freshness around the pitch. Gareth and Jason are preparing for their first games, Jonny hasn't played since the

Pumas, myself and Gavin Henson are paired together for only
the second time. And the coaches are different: Geech and
Gareth Jenkins with Mike Ford on defence. Lots of new
voices and energy. I came in and out of the session, swapping
with Shane Horgan, who is going to be on the bench on
Wednesday. Though I felt OK I was only just over twelve
hours away from finishing a torrid game.

We clapped and cheered as we came off. You do that
sometimes when things go well. That felt great. Back to the
hotel, where Louise Ramsey, God bless her, had realized that
I had barely had a moment to myself in the last twenty-four
hours: she had sent a bell boy up to my room to pack my bag
and bring it down to reception, where she checked me out.
A lovely touch and typical of the concern and effort everybody shows in this party. Then we headed for the airport,
and just when we needed everything to go smoothly we were
delayed on the tarmac for an hour. Nobody's fault, just an
air-traffic-control delay on a busy Sunday night. Until then I
had felt fine, but as we sat stewing on the runway I felt the
energy drain away from me. I wanted to sleep for ever and a
day but now I was captaining the Wednesday side a big press
conference awaited me at the Crown Plaza, Christchurch. We
wouldn't even start until 9 p.m. We got there and somehow I
stayed awake long enough to answer two very routine questions from the floor. There is a lot I would have liked to say
but I haven't got the energy to articulate it properly and the
press boys aren't in the mood for long in-depth stuff. They
are probably as tired as we are – if anything, they do even
more travelling than us because they are trying to be in two
places at the same time – and they just want to cover the
basics, file their stories and, I daresay, hit the sack themselves.
It will be asking a lot of Julian White to go again against

Wellington so soon after a massive match up front, but these are the crunch days of the tour and everybody is at full stretch in their own way.

I've been updating this journal on the hoof today. It has been very therapeutic, a great help in concentrating my mind and stopping me from fretting. Time for my cot now. Just so tired, can't think straight and can scarcely find the energy to talk. Down at the press conference I could hear myself slurring my words as if I've had one too many. Clive was the same; luckily for me, most of the questions were directed at him. This weekend has gone on for ever, it feels like a week or more. I am a lucky guy and lead a wonderful life but I feel like I'm really earning my wages at present. Expect we will get slammed here and back home tomorrow but I am past caring. They are only putting in print the disappointment we feel at ourselves. Will be nice to make them eat their words on Wednesday, though.

Just re-reading a nice email from Dad, spelling out that it is still early days and the Maori game was just a setback. Full of encouragement as usual. Even when I have played badly he finds something positive to pluck out of the game.

Monday 13 June, Crown Plaza Hotel

When in doubt, sleep. It's my remedy for most ills. I lay in until 11.30 and woke up feeling much more relaxed and less cranky. Today has been a good day off. Leisurely breakfast and then a stroll around Christchurch. On with my jeans, T-shirt, jacket, beanie hat and sunglasses. Plug into my iPod and I'm off into the wide world. You can only take so much of hotel rooms.

Christchurch is very peaceful. I'm sure it comes alive on rugby day, but it seems a little less full-on than the North Island. Walk around the city for a couple of hours shopping for a few presents back home, diving into coffee shops for a latte and to read the papers. Check out a couple of music shops for some new sounds – very good prices, about €11 for even the most expensive CDs. Also trying to think of something nice to buy Glenda when she comes over.

Just trying to re-create a quiet Monday morning in Dublin, doing the things I would do there. One or two people caught my eye and clearly clocked me but kept their distance and allowed me my privacy, which I am thankful for. Two Irish journalists hove into view – probably chilling in exactly the same way as myself. I took them by surprise when I called their names. Just for a second or two they hadn't recognized me. We passed the time of day pleasantly but briefly. All of us are looking for our own space. Touring is great, but it can drive you completely bonkers occasionally and you just have to go AWOL for a few hours.

Having got myself chilled and back in equilibrium, and at the precise moment when I started thinking it was time to go and find a little company, I bumped into Jason Robinson. Time for another coffee and a serious catch-up. Jason is a bit of a legend as far as I'm concerned. He's an incredible player, the model professional and a family man. His wife was having a difficult pregnancy – they have three children already – and it was clearly the right decision to let him stay home for a fortnight before joining the tour. He is happy, he has arrived with his mind clear and has immediately focused on the job. He looks in fantastic shape – he has obviously been training like a madman during his time at home – and it's a big boost after such a disappointing defeat to see him looking ready for

the fray. We have got a few aces to play yet. He was the
star turn at training on Sunday, and, unless I am mistaken,
Wednesday night in Wellington could turn into the Jason
Robinson show. He is in that kind of mood. All we have got
to do is feed him with quality ball. He and I had a good
natter. I am guessing it can be difficult for those arriving late
on tour – you can feel a little left out – so it was a pleasure
bringing him up to speed.

We went back to the team room. Nothing pinned up on
the board. We don't pin up any negative press, only the good,
so I can only assume we got an absolute panning back home.
The only other day the media guys pinned nothing up was
after the Pumas. I could look it up on the internet but I'm
not that interested. I know we played badly and have got to
improve. I also know that we can only do that by sticking
together and not overreacting to criticism. Beat Jason at table
tennis, but sure I'm in good form after three weeks out here,
he hasn't got his eye in yet. Nice to win, though.

After my glorious victory it was away to the masseurs
room, where I had booked in for the full monty, ninety
minutes of bliss. Because it was decided late on Saturday night
that I was playing this Wednesday I haven't allowed my body
to acknowledge that it is tired and bruised. Mentally I have
kept that at bay and will do until late on Wednesday night,
but of course deep down I am aching all over, which is why
I needed a world-class massage. Barty went into my shoulder,
which, as always, made it feel better. I am not allowing myself
to worry about the shoulder over much. It's a problem I live
with, it comes and goes.

I always prefer my massage late in the afternoon, it means
you can relax and float through the rest of the evening. Was
just thinking of retiring for a very early night when a bunch

of the lads marched in, having had a grand day messing about on the river on jetboats and darting above Christchurch in a helicopter. They seemed really animated and just for a minute I wondered perhaps if I should have gone with them. But no, I've had a fabulous day, and to each his own. I need to be on 'my time' on my day off, beholden to nobody. I'm not really into these activities, though I would love to get out for a few holes of golf some day soon.

Josh Lewsey, in contrast, is Mr Action Man. I'm sure the SAS will be giving him a call when he hangs his boots up. He will be the Lions security officer down here in twelve or twenty-four years' time. Others aren't far behind. Ben Kay will try anything once – I think he's already done the 400-foot bungee off the Sky Tower back in Auckland. We are not meant to go anywhere near that until the rugby is over, but I like the thought that we have people in this squad who will do their own thing occasionally.

Back to the boats. My spy – Gareth Thomas, the esteemed Wales captain – tells me that there was a funny moment when the press boat went skimming off the river out of control and ended up on a bank of shale. That in itself is obviously worth a wee chuckle, but then Geech and management, in another boat, went over to gloat and ended up stuck on a bank as well. He claims he went back because the press boys had the coffee and biscuits and he was freezing. If we had a court this would obviously incur hefty penalties, and I am filing it all away in the hope that we might yet get a court going. Mark Cueto would definitely be up in front of the judge as well. When some of the boys went off-piste on the 4x4 Landrovers last week, he nearly wiped out half our back division when he crashed and left the car about three inches from a rocky precipice. Even Josh was terrified and sweating buckets.

Just had a random thought flash through my mind: it's only nine days since our first game and Lawrence's injury, and here I am already writing and thinking about our fourth game on tour against Wellington. Everything is happening at a million miles an hour. The film is permanently on fast forward. That's why I just had to put it on hold today. Have made a little note to myself not to overdo the geeing-up over the next couple of days. There are a lot of experienced people in this party and they know the score. I will try and save my passionate stuff for the day of the game.

I really am heading for my bed now. Much happier with life than I was last night. Fortunes fluctuate very quickly on tour. A good solid win on Wednesday and we will be back on track.

PS. Forgot to tell you the Graham Rowntree incident. We were flying back from Hamilton last night and one of the air hostesses was fascinated by Graham's cauliflower ears, which, it has to be said, are spectacular in the extreme. She couldn't believe what she was seeing and – strange girl this – she asked if she could squeeze them. That would be my worst nightmare. Anyway, Graham hammed it up and let out a scream of agony when she squeezed and the poor girl recoiled in horror. Danny Grewcock, meanwhile, completely lost it when we landed, probably just exhausted like the rest of us. He was trying to get out of his seat, not realizing he still had his seat belt fastened. He couldn't work it out at all and was getting progressively more angry as he battled away. 'What the bloody hell's going on,' I could see him muttering to himself. Any more of that and I feared he might resort to his black belt karate skills and trash the seat, so I did the decent thing and freed him.

Tuesday 14 June, Christchurch, then Wellington

Just when I was getting used to the haka, in fact becoming a little blasé about the whole thing, it hit me right between the eyes again today after training down at Christchurch School, one of the most exclusive and best rugby schools in the country. It's a longstanding tradition for the school to issue the haka at least once when Lions tour parties use the ground. After our session ended the entire school – 600, maybe 700 pupils – lined the school's lovely quadrangle, which looks like something from one of the top Oxford colleges or Trinity College Dublin. They were all dressed in shorts, including the older boys aged seventeen or eighteen, and their First XV lined up in the middle of the quadrangle to lead the haka. Just for a second I thought this could be a little embarrassing and forced, but from the moment they started it was incredible. The acoustics were amazing, the chants and cries reverberated around the quadrangle. There could have been 6,000 rather than 600 kids and the lads had obviously been practising hard. They were totally together and in synch with their movements. When they stopped there was a sudden and complete silence – a noisy silence if you know what I mean – which nobody wanted to break. A stand-off just like you might get in the Tests. It was spine-chilling stuff and just heightened the feeling that, come the Tests, we will be taking on the nation. It's one thing being confronted by massive Maori warriors in their warpaint shouting their challenge – I have got used to that by now – but to see the young white

Our first defeat of the tour came against an excellent New Zealand Maori side – here I am kicking for touch with Carlos Spencer looking on, and scoring a consolation try with all my usual elegance.

I needed a lot of time to myself during the build-up to the first Test, but it was great to spend time with my sisters the evening before the match. The following evening, leaving the hotel for Jade Stadium, I was in the zone: I had never felt better.

Facing the haka before the first Test in Christchurch, with Dwayne Peel – our youngest warrior – by my side. We were very careful to accept the challenge in an appropriate fashion, and I was disgusted by suggestions to the contrary.

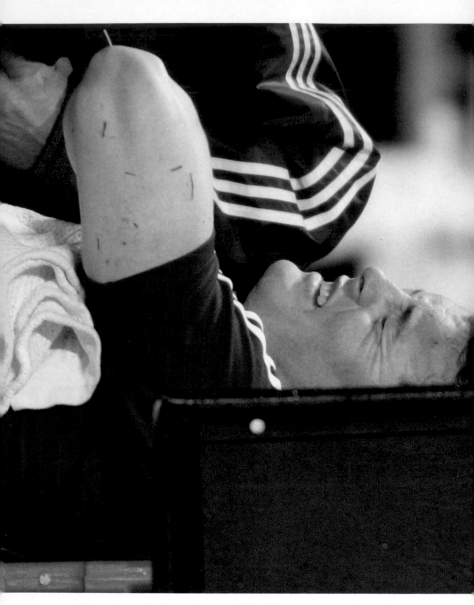

After less than a minute of play in the first Test, I was stretchered off with a dislocated right shoulder, having been slam-dunked by Keven Mealamu and Tana Umaga. The worst moment of my career.

I'm not a happy camper in the hotel lobby after being discharged from hospital. *Below*, Clive Woodward with the video evidence: Keven Mealamu has already got hold of my left leg, and Tana Umaga is about to grab the right.

With my shoulder crocked, facing the media was the biggest challenge remaining for me on the tour. The incident followed Tana, too, when fans unveiled a critical placard at an All Blacks training session.

Trying to smile my way through the final fortnight . . .
Failing with my new mate Willie (sorry, Prince William) but achieving
more success with Clive at Eden Park after the third and final Test.

A big night out in Auckland with Glenda and two of my best mates,
Damien and Ciaran.

Relaxing at home with my housemate Barry.

lads in their shorts and school blazers working up a head of steam, eyes bulging and tongues out, makes you realize yet again how much passion for the game there is down here. It was a great moment, very energizing. The disappointment of the Maori game is quickly receding. If we dwell on things down here we will be lost.

After training we headed off for Wellington and the Intercontinental Hotel, which we will be getting to know well in a couple of weeks when we play the second Test. Everything moved up a couple of notches today. Players were sharper in training and there seems an edge here in Wellington. The hotel is cordoned off with barriers outside and there are fans waiting almost around the clock to pounce for autographs when we nip out – and the first Test is still ten days away. Comments in the press are becoming much harsher on both sides.

Have just been told there is an absolute nonsense story running in the *Daily Mail* and some other papers back home about a training-ground fight between Gordon Bulloch and John Hayes which left Gordon needing a few stitches. 'Tour in Crisis' apparently. All very attention-grabbing, except absolutely none of it is true. There wasn't a fight. The boys were practising their rucking and Gordon caught a boot and took a nick and the catgut was needed. It happens at training somewhere in Britain and Ireland every day of the week from August through to May. It is so common as not even to be worthy of comment. And yes, there are occasional fights or dust-ups between lifelong friends and colleagues. It's a physical sport and as big matches approach emotions run high. But for the record, there was no incident between Gordon and John. And even if there had been a few snarls, I wouldn't be the slightest bit worried.

What perplexes me is why a paper should run such a story without checking the facts. One phone call and any confusion could have been cleared up. I remember the day before the tour party was announced one paper categorically announced that Matt Dawson had been excluded. That's a pretty big statement to go public with unless you have checked your facts.

All a bit depressing. I would expect something like that from some New Zealand journalists in the run-up to the Tests – they have a different agenda and the Lions are considered fair game – but not from the travelling press. They don't have to be fans and supporters, just a fair crack of the whip would be nice.

It's irritating, but it will only become an issue if we allow it to be an issue, so unless specifically asked about it I am keeping my mouth firmly shut. Don't want to get diverted by anybody or anything at the moment. Feeling good and have recovered from Saturday quicker than I thought possible. My fitness level is at an all-time high.

Wednesday 15 June, Wellington

Just back from the match. High time for a very relaxing stroll! Our last opportunity before the Test. Have got twenty minutes before we meet in the lobby and head out, so thought I would write a few notes first.

Generally pleased with tonight's win. They were basically a tough Super 12 team minus their All Blacks and even in the filthy conditions we could have put forty points on them with a little more luck and precision with our final passes. I will settle for the narrower victory we got, though I wish we could have shown more of a killer instinct.

The weather was rubbish. Swirling, gusting wind with lots of rain. It cost us a fair few points tonight. Jonny kicked well given the conditions; the two goal-kicks he missed were by just a whisker. Neil Back made a tackle and turned them over direct from the start, and went on to have a fine first half.

Gethin Jenkins had an awesome game and clinched his Test place, not that there was any doubt really. His scrummaging was good, he got around the pitch like a flanker and his try was high quality. Dwayne Peel broke off the back of a line-out, found Martin Corry up in support on the inside, and Gethin finished it off from 20 yards out. Suspect one or two New Zealanders might have revised their opinion of us a little after seeing that. There is no substitute for class, and that was a very classy moment.

The big talking point from the game, of course, was taking Gavin Henson off after the hour, switching Jonny to inside centre alongside me and bringing on Stephen Jones at fly-half. Was our secret finally out or were we just trying a few variations and giving Stephen more game time? Nobody really knew except us. Moving Jonny was a strong possibility that Clive, the coaches and I had discussed since we first met up in Wales, and now we were dipping our toe in the water. Mind games if you like, but why not? Anything to confuse the All Blacks, although they have got such a wealth of experience among their coaches I am sure they have worked out that playing Jonny at 12 wouldn't be the strangest thing at all. Wayne Smith, their backs coach, has got a sharp rugby brain, and I am sure I read an article a while back where he suggested as much. Over here they see the fly-half and inside-centre roles as being much more closely related anyway. Their regular inside centre Aaron Mauger fits that mould perfectly.

That's enough for now, it's time for a little team bonding. We deserve that relaxing stroll. It's been a very tough week at the office, but I can feel the pressure easing a little.

Thursday 16 June, Christchurch

Very good night in Wellington – late but not too stupid. Rehab in the pool plus the usual ice plunges in the morning before flying back to Christchurch at lunchtime. Good to be back – it's beginning to feel like home, just like Auckland did. Went straight to training and we did a full session with Jonny alongside me at centre and Stephen Jones at fly-half. Everything seemed to click nicely. Jonny is a very special player and can adapt to most things. Playing outside him could be a lot of fun; we will gel very quickly. And of course putting Jonny at 12 means we can play the Welsh Grand Slam half-backs together. Looking at it from that angle, the Lions get the best of the deal. The only person who would really disagree would be Gavin, and it is going to be tough on him. He has played well so far and was very disappointed to be replaced last night. These are the tough decisions coaches have to make. Glad I only add my input and don't have to make the call.

We have decided to change our line-out calls because they are too simple for the opposition to break. Listened in for a minute to the new ones and they seemed over-complicated to me. It's none of my business – the forwards are the experts and I would take it badly if they started lecturing me on centre three-quarter play and calls in the back division. The line-out is key in modern rugby, the primary source of quality possession. We have got to get it right in the Tests.

Away from the rugby I can't really believe what's happening around me today. I was talking to Ray, one of our three regular security men, and he casually said: 'Have you noticed anything different today, Brian?'

I had a look around and a good think and couldn't think of anything in particular.

'We've had another three or four security guys with us since the start of the week,' he said, 'except they are undercover – they are so good you won't even know they are here. No point trying to see who they are because you will never guess.'

I was really taken aback. Lions against All Blacks is a pretty big deal, with thousands of supporters milling around, and I would be stupid not to think there could be something of a security risk. A determined terrorist could cause a fair amount of damage. But then Clive is also concerned about the security element in relation to the All Blacks. He is absolutely convinced that New Zealand have got spies in the camp, so to speak, and that there could be seven or eight waiters and chambermaids listening in on what we say and going through our wastepaper bins looking for scribbled notes on our plays and such. Clive thinks that the All Blacks would be well capable of setting up such an operation. Not quite sure I would buy into that. I know that before we go into any new hotel the security men go in and sweep it for bugs and phone taps, and Clive has spoken to us a couple of times on the need for vigilance at all times. Certainly, there does always seem to be some member of staff who suddenly finds something urgent to do in your vicinity! Am I getting paranoid?

No, I'm not imagining it. I am trying to write this down in a quiet corner of the lobby and have had to move twice in the last twenty minutes.

To be honest I just don't know what to make of it. Everything seems just too incredible for words. I suppose industrial espionage is a fact of life all over the world so there is no reason why a multi-million-pound business like international rugby should be any different.

There was definitely a thought four years ago in Australia that the Wallabies had somehow got hold of our line-out calls and that that cost us dear in the third Test when Martin Johnson, of all people, lost a few balls that you would ordinarily expect him to gobble up. The theory then is that one of the waterboys on the touchline had a tape device and used to station himself by every line-out and record our calls. The Aussie technical team would then match that up with video footage of where the ball actually went!

What I do know is that we now have all our meetings in the 'War Room' as opposed to the team room. The War Room is where we store our game plans, notes on back moves and line-outs, etc. We never take anything out of the War Room and it is guarded twenty-four hours a day.

Clive could be absolutely right – it could be a very necessary precaution. Or it could be that there is no security threat whatsoever – and Clive knows that – but he wants to promote the idea that there is something going on and create a bunker mentality which can bring the team and squad together. Or perhaps it's a complete load of nonsense.

Going in on yourself, in a situation like this, is natural, I suppose. I notice now that I am less likely to do any autographs and shirt-signings in the hotel. When I am in Lions kit on official business I am fair game, to a certain extent, and if somebody notices me out in the streets or a coffee bar that's OK as long as they are polite. But the team hotel – no matter which one – is my home away from home and I would be just as angry if anyone came banging on my door at number 35 just before midnight expecting autographs.

It probably says a good deal for my very mellow state of mind at present that none of this seems to be alarming me or upsetting my sense of equilibrium. It's as if I am somebody else and the momentous events and strange happenings of this tour are actually happening to another person called Brian O'Driscoll. I am not explaining myself very well – I will have another go tomorrow when I feel a bit brighter.

Friday 17 June, Crown Plaza, Christchurch

Just rereading my last paragraph from last night and think I finally know what I am trying to say. Ever since we arrived down here I've been like a different person. Barry said something to that effect a couple of weeks ago when we chatted briefly on the phone. I have become very insular and – to use an overused but appropriate word – focused. Since we touched down my world doesn't exist outside of the Lions, the hotel room we are staying in, the pitch we are playing on, the restaurant we are eating in or, occasionally, the bar we are drinking in. It has become my life – I feel totally consumed by the Lions – and for the time being I cannot allow anything to intrude on that life or prick the bubble in which I am living. It requires my total concentration and if, on my day off for example, there is nothing pressing to do, then that is my time and I don't want anybody interfering with that either. After starting off full of good intentions, I have become a bit lax about ringing and mailing home. This is something I need to go through alone, even though at a very basic level it is the love and support of those closest to me that inspire me.

I read an interesting article the other day in which Colin Meads – who toured the world with the All Blacks for months or even years on end – said that he never phoned home when away. Apparently he and his then fiancée – now his wife for well over forty years – had a blazing row on the phone when he was away in Australia and decided thereafter that they would only ever communicate by letter, twice a week. I know exactly how they came to that decision. You have to be free to live in your world when you are away.

After thinking it would be nice for Glenda to come out for the fortnight, I am now dead set against it. I can't be giving her the attention she deserves in and around Test weeks. How can I tell her that I don't fancy a quiet meal out or that I would rather go for a walk in the park on my own in my spare time? I am always quite selfish when I am preparing for a big match, and now the biggest games of my life are on the horizon. Actually I am amazed how many players seem to be easy about having wives and partners around in the build-up to a big match. I suppose it is a little different if you are married or live with somebody and are used to all their moods, but I am unliveable-with in the twenty-four hours leading up to a game – totally self-centred. I must be old-fashioned but I couldn't possibly share a bed with a partner before a big game. I might want to get up at 2 a.m. and go for a walk, read a book or wake up the masseur for a rub-down! I might be up for breakfast at 9 a.m. but I might want to sleep until much later and have brunch in bed, especially for late-evening kick-offs like the ones on this tour.

I have to be totally free to do exactly what I want to do and catering for nobody else until the moment comes when I slip into captaincy mode. Am I a bit odd? I don't think so. If I look at myself objectively, my strongest quality as a rugby player is to concentrate totally on the job in hand. I am not the biggest, fastest, strongest – though I have good physical attributes – but not many people want it more than me.

My parents are arriving in Christchurch on the day of the match, but I have got no idea whether I will see them before we head off to Wellington on the Sunday afternoon. I just cannot get tied up with the logistics of maybe trying to arrange a hook-up at the moment. We will catch up when we catch up, when the time is right, and it will be lovely and meaningful. Their support and love is there, like it has always been, and that is the only thing that matters. The texts and emails keep coming in, and I am never left in any doubt that they are thinking of me. After the tour I will spoil them and Glenda, but until then I am putting number one first.

Hope some of that makes sense. Thought it important that I at least try and get it down on paper. No doubt the sports psychologists will recognize all sorts of disastrous and disturbing character traits.

On a less philosophical note the local papers down here on the South Island are far from happy that we have cancelled a few engagements down at Dunedin over the weekend. We can't please everybody all of the time, there is a Test series to try and win. It's part of that going-in-on-yourself business I was trying to explain above.

Good session today, with Jonny lining up at inside centre alongside me. He is almost the archetypal old-style inside centre in build and qualities, it's just that he has played most of his rugby at outside half.

Saturday 18 June, airborne, Dunedin–Christchurch

Flying back from Dunedin to Christchurch after our win against Otago. Very quiet on the plane – just a few management and players, the rest are staying in Dunedin for a few beers and some community work tomorrow. Can make out the Southern Alps out to my left under the strong moonlight. It's a beautiful country. We don't have that much time to appreciate it, but everywhere we go and everything we do seems to be played out against a spectacular backdrop.

We are all tired and lost in our own thoughts, looking ahead to next Saturday. Wonder what our emotions will be exactly a week from now after the first Test. Feeling nervous just at the thought of it, but there is a long way to go yet and a busy week of training. We have been preparing and thinking about next week for a long time, yet it still seems that there is barely enough time to fit everything in.

I wasn't sure whether I should travel down to Dunedin or not – most of the non-playing squad, i.e. the majority of those who will make up the Test team, have stayed behind in Christchurch for a rest or to get treatment for knocks – but I thought it important to display some solidarity with the lads and to show my face generally, given the negative press we have been getting down here for postponing a couple of community visits. You can't win, really. We have made a big effort on this tour but as the Tests loom large you have to be a little bit flexible. We didn't cancel everything wholesale, just rejigged things so that those who are definitely going to be involved in the first Test can get some quality training together and rest time.

Thought the 30–19 win over Otago was very encouraging,

given that it was essentially our 'second' team on view. Gordon Bulloch led the side well and they pulled away impressively in the second half. There was a great buzz in the changing room afterwards, the sort you only get occasionally. Often, if you haven't played, you feel out of it, but afterwards it felt like I had been out there myself. The feel-good factor continued through to the post-match press conference, which was broadcast live on New Zealand TV. Clive and Ian McGeechan were very upbeat – Clive said he 'had a warm feeling about this squad' and could 'feel something special happening', and Geech smiled when he was told that Otago's captain Craig Newby had accused us of 'cheating like buggery' at the breakdown. 'I think we must getting something right in that case,' replied Geech. You have to meet fire with fire down here. It's the only language they understand and respect.

The major talking point of the game was a stunning debut for Ryan Jones at number 8. Ryan was called up as a replacement when Simon Taylor went home. He flew in last week from Canada, where he was touring with Wales. His impact has been amazing. He is very fresh and raw – in a good sense, not constrained by too much coaching – and he is extremely relaxed and grounded as a guy. Apparently he walked into the press conference eating pizza and held court for twenty minutes. It can't be easy being parachuted into a close-knit squad, but he has taken it all in his long stride. He was magnificent out there tonight – so strong and direct going forward and tough and hard-working in defence. He scored one try after good work by Shane Williams and then made another for Shane after showing the confidence to tap and go from inside the Lions' half and run hard at Otago. He was rightly named man of the match and is clearly now a contender for the Test pack. A star was born tonight. Got a feeling Ryan is going to be a major player for Wales for years to come.

Shane Williams did well and comes back into Test contention, and Will Greenwood had a fine match – perhaps he sensed it was his night when the ball stood up nicely from Charlie Hodgson's excellent cross-field kick for a try just before half-time. Thought Simon Easterby had another excellent match, probably second only to Ryan, and I've heard more than one comment along the lines of 'Why weren't they here in the first place and how come, in this most prepared squad of all time, the two best players on the night are those who joined the party late?' Valid questions. Both Ryan and Simon were very close to making the original squad, that's why they were on stand-by. And I suppose that extra motivation of being determined to prove the selectors wrong comes into play when they eventually make their debuts. Clive's squad system is very easy to slot into. Everything is meticulously organized and is now running at full throttle.

Sunday 19 June, Christchurch

Have been pondering this morning's thought of the day, contributed by Eddie O'Sullivan. 'Why do kamikaze pilots wear crash helmets?' It's probably just another one of Eddie's little phrases, but is there a deeper hidden meaning we are meant to pick up on? Wish I could think of a witty reply for when I bump into him next. Best sleep of the tour last night. Dead to the world until gone noon and felt a million dollars when I got up – except for my dodgy left shoulder. Just another three weeks to go, I know I can get through it. If I need an operation or some prolonged rehab after that it doesn't matter. Just get me through the next three weeks, please.

Big crunch meeting tonight with the announcement of the Southland and Test sides. The moment everybody looks forward to but also dreads. First Clive read out the team to play Southland – those who wouldn't be in the Test reckoning – and there were some very hurt faces. Gavin Henson, who has done almost nothing wrong. Geordan Murphy, Charlie Hodgson, Chris Cusiter and Gordon Bulloch likewise. The last two have flown the Scottish flag with distinction and been exemplary tourists. Clive and Geech told the team that they would define the tour and that their contribution this week – at the game and at training – was vital. Words like that sound good and are well intentioned, but they mean very little to the players they are aimed at. Clive then asked the Southland squad to leave the room, and I expect many of the lads took themselves off to their rooms for a shout and a few tears. I found it very emotional that to a man they were so gutted not to have made the Test squad, and this has only reinforced my determination that we won't let them down next Saturday.

Which left just twenty-three of us and the coaches. Clive revealed the team and replacements by drawing back one of those big pages on his drawing board. There was one either/ or – Shane Williams or Shaggy on the bench. I quickly glanced at the twenty-three faces staring intently at the board and they were completely rapt. No hollering or shouting. This is a bright group of people and most of them had guessed by our training formations on Friday and Saturday morning which way the wind was blowing. I caught Shaggy's eye for a moment and he was ablaze. He wanted that last slot on the bench so badly. New Year's Eve in Cork seemed a very long way away. We have been through so much together that I could easily guess exactly how he was thinking.

So the team. A back three of Jason Robinson, Josh Lewsey and Gareth Thomas, with Jason nominally at full-back, though we have plans to swap and switch. Jonny and myself at centre. The Welsh boys Stephen Jones and Dwayne Peel at half-back. Gethin Jenkins, Shane Byrne and Julian White in the front row, Paul O'Connell and Ben Kay at lock, and a tough, experienced English back-row trio of Richard Hill, Neil Back and Martin Corry.

I had known the team for a day or two but that didn't detract one jot from a special moment. I looked at Hillie and knew how pleased he was. Nine months ago his career could have been over, yet he had battled back, as I knew he would, and looks very fit. He doesn't appear to get excited too often – reserved and very English – but I know from conversations with him that the prospect of this very moment was the one that has kept him going since he wrecked his knee in October. Martin has been a tower of strength since Lawrence left, stepping up as the pack leader. And Backie showed against Wellington that he has not quite finished yet. He will be head to head with Richie McCaw, one of the greats as far as I'm concerned – but Backie is one of the few opponents in world rugby that McCaw would spend any time worrying about.

Delighted for Paul. Now he has made the Test team we will see the very best of him. Can't help but think he has felt under pressure since being labelled the 'new Martin Johnson', which would do anybody's head in. He will kick on now. Ben Kay has been in good form since we arrived. A very bright man, Ben, he's enjoyed the whole circus of touring, takes it all in his stride.

Not sure how the public and the scribes will react. Other than the moving of Jonny to 12 and the fact that Gavin didn't make the bench I don't think there can be too many arguments. Jason is short of rugby, and I was hoping things would run his way against Wellington last week, but he has enough class and pedigree to justify a start, and it makes sense to go with the tried and tested combination at half-back.

Finally went back to relax in my room and switched on the TV for the finale of *Dancing with the Stars*. Norm Hewitt was brilliant again and I texted in a couple of votes to try and make sure a rugby man won the title, which he did.

'The rugby vote came through again,' said Norm afterwards. 'I was just ahead with the judges, but the audience vote can turn it, and Sean always does well on that. I know a stack of Lions supporters were voting for me, so thanks for that. I am very proud. I like to think I have helped make dancing OK for guys again.'

Must text Keith Wood and see if he fancies it for the BBC in their next series of *Strictly Come Dancing*.

Monday 20 June, Christchurch

Some of the papers are full of praise for the lads visiting a children's hospital down in Dunedin the day after the match, with a cracking picture of Gordon D'Arcy laughing his head off while holding a small baby. Perhaps we are not so awful after all. Good to see Darce in good form. He has had a tough tour, it just hasn't happened for him. He hasn't played enough rugby over the past year and now his confidence has dipped a bit, which creates a vicious circle. The harder you try, the more tensed up and less confident you become. He will be back.

Lots of excitement and speculation about the Test team by media and supporters. Most of them seem to have read the tea leaves correctly, with widespread agreement that Jonny will be playing 12 with Stephen Jones at fly-half and an all-English back row. Nobody to my knowledge has worked out that we will have Jason Robinson at full-back and Josh Lewsey on the wing.

Beautiful weather here in Christchurch, clear and crisp and quite warm around lunchtime. Perfect for training. So far so good.

Have finally, definitely, decided that Glenda isn't going to fly out. Just can't handle anything else except the rugby at present.

Tuesday 21 June, Christchurch

Just watched the Tuesday team scrape a win down at Southland. Disappointed, it was comfortably our worst display on tour, just when I was hoping they would give everybody a big lift. It's easy for me to pontificate because I am lucky enough to have been selected for the Test, but the lads just reacted in the wrong way to not making the cut. They took out their anger by playing as individuals, with everybody trying too hard. They needed, more than ever, to operate as a team and just take care of the basics. If they had stuck to that and built a lead by half-time they would have crushed Southland in the second half. Instead, they became involved in a dogfight, and it needed two sharply taken tries by Gavin

Henson to pull us through. It's really tough for the lads, I'm feeling guilty just writing these words, but I was looking for much more tonight. I wanted the squad and the supporters to be on the crest of a wave going into the Test.

Scott Johnson, Wales's Australian backs coach, has just arrived as an observer for the Lions and had an interesting experience at Immigration after getting off the plane. Scott, you may remember, achieved a certain notoriety last November when he called New Zealand 'just a poxy little island in the Pacific' amidst the war of words ahead of Wales's game against the All Blacks at the Millennium Stadium. Snubbed Kiwis have long memories, as Scott has just been telling us.

'I presented my passport at the desk and after the girl typed my number into the computer she looked a little concerned and went to fetch a supervisor,' he said. 'I stood around for a long time getting increasingly concerned and feeling terrible when finally this huge guy wandered over with my passport in his hand. He then made a big play of inspecting the passport in minute detail.'

'Ah, Mr Johnson, we have been looking forward to your arrival for some time,' said the Immigration officer, before breaking into a massive smile. 'A thousand welcomes to our poxy little island in the Pacific. I do hope your stay with us isn't too awful.'

Had a chat with Gethin Jenkins today, and he was telling me his mum, Lesley, is out here with a group of family and friends despite being diagnosed with lung cancer last year. She had already booked the trip when she was diagnosed, long before Gethin had been named in the tour squad. She has been having chemotherapy treatment but has suspended the course for a month to come out here. I don't know who will be the most proud on Saturday – Gethin of his mum or Lesley of Gethin.

Wednesday 22 June, Christchurch

Big team announcement in the town hall opposite our hotel this evening. Live on New Zealand TV – big musical fanfare as we walked in, and Lions highlights on the big screen. Over the top. You can set yourself up for a fall with stuff like this. Bit of a comic moment when we come to the twenty-two empty chairs that had been cleared for the team and squad – one of the journos thought it would be fun to take a couple of them away so there was a bit of a scrap for the last couple of spaces!

Clive explained our team selections well enough. As we trooped back out and past the camera, Paul O'Connell couldn't resist the chance to make mischief and pulled Alastair Campbell's tracksuit bottoms down around his ankles. You can be the world's best-known spin doctor, but nothing can stop a middle-aged man with his tracksuit around his ankles looking anything other than plain ridiculous.

Another good day's training. Still seems to be some debate about the line-out calls. I thought that was sorted last week. Weather is still holding, but the forecast is for a big south-westerly to hit Christchurch on Saturday evening. New Zealand weather forecasts are normally as inaccurate and fallible as those in most other places in the world, but this one seems very specific. We will see.

Thursday 23 June, Christchurch

Nervous. Normal day off. Slept until nearly midday, brunch, walked around town with ROG and Denis Hickie. I dressed up in my normal jeans, jacket and beanie, but my disguise was ruined by the others having no hats and wearing their Lions stash. No worries. We stopped and chatted with the punters and generally wasted the day away. Crashed on my bed early evening, dozing and reading my book. Then a meal with a few of the lads, back to the room, read and listen to music. Not wonderfully exciting, but exactly what I wanted to do.

Friday 24 June, Crown Plaza, Christchurch

Walk-through at the Jade Stadium. Still gorgeous weather but the wet stuff is definitely on the way. Could even be snow, so the local pundits say. Whatever. Rugby is a game played in the elements, and I love it like that. I don't care what we get.

Just scribbling this before going to sleep. Feel very calm and completely together after a slight attack of the jitters yesterday. Had an enjoyable catch-up with my sisters and Jules's fiancé Tomás tonight, and they were just the ideal company. They know all my moods and wouldn't get upset if I suddenly wanted to go off for a stroll for half an hour or go to bed half-way through a meal. And of course, because I am relaxed and happy, I don't do any of those things! They have been having a great time on tour with all the campervan supporters up and down the South Island.

We have to hit New Zealand with everything tomorrow evening. They should be a little rusty after seven months without a major game and we have to make that count. And as for me, I've never felt better or more ready. I can feel a huge game inside me and I want to deliver. Tomorrow is the most important day of my rugby life. I want to relish every second of being the Lions captain in a Test match. It will be hard and testing but that's how I like it. My shoulder has stopped hurting – it could just be mind over matter – but I don't care, I feel ready for action.

Aftermath

Sunday 26 June, Inter-Continental Hotel

Recording this into a dictaphone now because I can't write or even dress myself properly at the moment. Feel bloody helpless, like a baby. Expect I will get used to it. My golfing holiday in July is up the spout, that's for sure. Still wide awake – my shoulder is too painful for sleep – and determined to tell you everything about this weekend while it is fresh in my mind.

Keven Mealamu and Tana Umaga dislocated my shoulder yesterday – they could have broken my neck for all they seemed to care – and my reign as Lions Test captain lasted exactly forty-one seconds. It's been a complete disaster personally, and I am still so angry I want to lash out at somebody with my one good arm.

The New Zealand haka first. From the very start of the tour we had discussed, at some length, how to accept the haka before the Test, because for the All Blacks that's clearly where the game begins. Also, you can encounter a haka at almost any time before or after a game in New Zealand. We have bent over backwards to do everything by the book on this tour and not to upset any Maori or New Zealand sensibilities. This is their country, we are visitors and we are trying to do the right thing. So when we discussed how to accept the haka at the first Test, Clive mentioned a number of emails he had received on the subject, including one from a Maori elder which detailed exactly how it should be done with the maximum of respect. These instructions were consistent with advice we received from the Maori welcoming party all those weeks ago in Rotorua.

We followed his plan to the letter. I, as the warrior chief, stepped forward directly opposite their chief – Tana Umaga – to accept the challenge, accompanied, as best practice dictates, by our youngest warrior, Dwayne Peel. The rest of the team fanned out across the pitch and remained as motionless as Easter Island statues. It was an exhilarating moment.

As protocol demands, I tried to maintain eye contact with Tana and remain still, even though it was freezing cold and I could feel muscles tightening up, especially my hamstring, which I always like to keep warm in the immediate build-up to the game. I normally keep my tracksuit bottoms on during the anthems back home and sometimes have the masseur run on and work on my hamstring there and then. But we decided to bin that to avoid any possible misinterpretation.

Tana always seems to get pretty worked up when he leads the haka – it's an incredible advantage for the All Blacks to perform it while their opponents stand there subservient and powerless – but it's part of the tradition and a Lions tour is about maintaining tradition. But this time he seemed to be particularly animated and hyped up.

When the haka was finished it was time to formally accept the challenge. As the Maori elder in the email had instructed, I leaned forward while still maintaining eye contact, clutched a piece of grass from the pitch and threw it to the wind. It went properly, thank God. Tana, though, was still looking extremely agitated.

I've subsequently been told that some of the All Blacks and

spectators thought we had insulted them by the manner in which we received the haka. That is just too incredible for words. We had done our homework thoroughly and made every effort to ensure we behaved in textbook fashion, and now I have to put up with this crap. The truth is that at Christchurch on Saturday night we understood and respected the haka a little bit better than some of the All Blacks and many of their camp followers and media who have been whinging today. What more do they want from us?

They have to show us respect as well. If it's a problem with us smiling or twitching at the wrong time – as has been suggested – there is a very simple solution. We can do away with the haka. Then we can't possibly offend anybody and we can all start on a level playing field.

Anyway, the match kicked off, and the All Blacks pressed hard right from the whistle. After about thirty seconds I was involved in a tackle on Leon MacDonald. The All Blacks were favourites to win the ball – Leon laid it back well – and Jerry Collins formed the perfect protective bridge. I was on my feet and started leaning and pushing on Jerry – counter-bridging is what all the coaches call it – in the probably vain hope that I might just be able to nudge Jerry into Justin Marshall and slightly spoil their possession. It was a completely routine situation – New Zealand were recycling the ball as per textbook – but it was the first minute of a Test series and the adrenalin was running high.

Suddenly I was aware of their hooker, Keven Mealamu, trying to pick me up by my left leg. Giving him the benefit of the doubt, he might have considered the ruck to be live and have been trying, in New Zealand fashion, to 'clear' me out. Completely illegal of course, but commonplace down here and condoned by the refs even if those same refs immediately blow for a penalty if the All Blacks are trying it on in the northern hemisphere.

No alarm bells yet. I am a solid 14 stone plus and had a good strong body position, so initially Mealamu struggled to shift me. On my right, Tana Umaga joined the action on our side of the ruck and was fringing around a little, blocking any Lions attempt to get to the ball and generally waiting to see how things developed. He was facing infield towards the Lions, having driven through the ruck. He swivelled to the left as Marshall cleared the ball, and then swivelled back to me and got busy, grabbing me high on my right leg and lifting. Again I tried to resist, but Mealamu was still at it as well, and this time I felt myself coming off the ground, with the ball already in Dan Carter's hands.

This was really serious and dangerous. I felt extremely vulnerable: I had never been upended like that before in a rugby match. I could hear Gareth Thomas screaming to the touch judge, Andrew Cole, who had stepped into the field of play. I could also hear Cole shouting: 'Leave him alone, put him down, put him down.' They certainly did that: they dumped me from a great height and I found myself heading for the ground more quickly than seemed natural. Was I speared? I think so. Slam-dunked is probably the expression which sums it up the best. Not that it makes much difference – even if they just dropped me they were reckless as to whether I broke my neck or not.

As I was thrown down, the only thing in my mind was to somehow break my fall. Much better to break my hand or my arm than my neck. I stretched out with my right arm just in time and hit the ground with a thud. The pain was instantaneous. Something had to give and it was my right shoulder, which had sheared away and, as I now know, dislocated. I tried to shout out to Andrew Cole, who I could still sense standing by the ruck, but I had no voice at all – either I had been winded or the shock had numbed me for a minute. I felt like a drowning man, I wanted to shout for help but nobody could hear me. Play had moved to the far side of the pitch and I was stranded.

The Lions fans by the touchline were going berserk and Gareth sprinted down the touchline, oblivious to play, to remonstrate with Andrew Cole, who now seemed to have forgotten his earlier intervention. Eventually play stopped somewhere over the other side of the field, I believe we stopped the All Blacks just short of the line. I was in agony but I thought it might pass – a stinger, hopefully, like the injury that affects my other shoulder, or just a badly jarred nerve. But the searing pain got worse. The Lions physio, Phil Pask, was quickly with me and after a quick examination started talking into his walkie-talkie: 'Suspected dislocated shoulder, cart needed.'

In an instant I knew my tour was over and I could immediately feel the tears coming. Phil and his colleague, my cousin Gary, tried to put the shoulder back in there and then, but it wouldn't budge. It was time to get me off the pitch and into the medical room. I was sweating profusely with the shock and trauma despite the freezing conditions.

The cart was completely hopeless, an old-fashioned stretcher would have been much better. I could feel every bump and rut in the field. It was the worst moment of my life. I felt embarrassed and pathetic being paraded the long way around the ground before I could get into the medical room. I could see all these Lions fans looking as stunned as I felt. Bizarrely, I wanted them to stop the cart so I could apologize to them personally. The party hadn't even begun and I was on the way home. I wanted to wind the clock back just three minutes and start again. Why was this happening to me? I felt completely cheated.

Of all the New Zealanders, only Justin Marshall was concerned enough at the fate of a fellow professional rugby player to come over and ask how I was and give me a comforting pat at the lowest point of my rugby career. Justin is a very tough, some would say spiky, customer, who I've always rated as a player; but much more importantly I now rate him as a bloke. He had the decency to separate himself from the All Black herd and do the right thing, and as soon as this mess is over I will try to seek him out and say thank you over a beer.

The medical room was chaos. A spectator had collapsed – and subsequently died, I am sad to say – so initially there was no morphine, as the supply had been taken up into the stand to try to help him. Much the same thing happened to Lawrence when he injured his ankle versus Bay of Plenty – the New Zealand authorities at Rotorua had no morphine readily available and Lawrence had to wait fifty minutes.

They stretched me out on the table and the stadium nurse/physio, I am not sure exactly what she was, started to cut my Lions shirt off. I had never known pain like it. To help the pain until they could find some more morphine a medic started using laughing gas on me, except that he almost suffocated me putting it down my throat. I pushed it away and asked for him to just hold it above my mouth, and it eased things slightly.

Then, and I still can't believe this, the nurse asked me if she could have my Lions shirt. Mother of God, what was she thinking? I've been speared off the bloody pitch after just forty seconds of the Test series and she wants the shirt off my back as well. Picking over the bones of the Lions corpse. I tried to use some very bad language but the words wouldn't come. Still she persisted. She had a couple of kids and they would love it. Brian O'Driscoll, the Lions number 13 shirt on the evening he was booted out of the first Test. Get this woman out of here, I was thinking, still unable to talk properly. What is wrong with this bloody country? Just start treating me like a human being, will you? Nobody will ever have this shirt. It's the only tangible thing I have got that says I captained the 2005 Lions in a Test match. Through no fault of my own I have been denied any other memories.

Luckily Dad had fought his way through security by now and sensed exactly what I was agitated about. He took a firm hold of the shirt as it and my undershirt came off. It was in safe hands.

Eventually the chief medic found some morphine and injected me. Then, instead of waiting a few minutes for it to kick in, he started yanking away immediately to try to get the shoulder back in. Will this torture never end? Please, somebody do something for the pain, I'm going to pass out. Out of the corner of my eye something was happening. Richard Hill was being helped into the changing room. His knee has gone again, poor bugger; he had tried so hard to get back for this tour. He was led away to the changing room next door while I was screaming my head off. It must have been unpleasant for him to listen to, but Richard is as steady as a rock, he doesn't get fazed by much. And I expect he was deep in his own misery.

Finally, finally, finally, the shoulder crunched back in – there was a moment of pain that nearly caused me to black out and then the pure bliss of feeling it come right again. Painful, but not that screeching, vomit-inducing pain. I had been sweating like a pig, but that immediately stopped.

Went to hospital for an X-ray, which mercifully revealed no break. Felt completely out of it as the morphine took hold properly, all a bit too late really. Then went back to the hotel and made a point of attending the team meeting. I started the day as a member of the Lions team and I was buggered if I was going to end the day on my own in bed under sedation.

We lost the match 21–3, and the boys were very down, but they were fantastic to me. Players instinctively know when something is wrong or right. And they knew that I had been done in cold blood.

Later I met up with the family. They have always been there for me and now, true to form, here they are in Christchurch taking the strain. The two girls were emotional, particularly Jules, and had been crying buckets, though they were trying hard not to blub in front of their little brother. We just sat around in a sad little corner having a bite to eat and a cup of tea. Three or four times I just caught Dad's eye and we just shook our heads in unison. At one stage it was just him and me together for a minute and he was as angry as I have ever seen him, but when the girls came back or there was any company he was poised and composed. No way was he going to lose it in public.

About 2 a.m., or perhaps a little later, the extraordinary news came through that the South African citing commissioner Willem Venter – a lawyer with little rugby experience – had refused to cite the two All Blacks, which would have involved taking a proper look at the incident and interviewing those closest to it – i.e. me, Keven Mealamu, Tana Umaga, Andrew Cole and Gareth Thomas. The referee, Joel Jutge, wasn't that far away either, but he was following the ball and I would be surprised if he really saw the incident. It makes no sense. We also heard that the citing officer was intending to fly home first thing this morning. Why the rush? Why aren't these things looked at properly in the sober light of day? The match is barely over. The Lions and All Blacks have got two Test matches to play yet. Why is he in such a rush to get home? Not for the first time it seems virtually impossible to cite a New Zealand player in New Zealand. Ali Williams sliced open Josh Lewsey's face with a kick two years ago – twenty-five stitches, was it? – but nothing was seen. Ian Jones nearly took Graham Rowntree's head off in 1998, but of course nothing was ever done.

The media from both camps were inundating us with calls for a statement so eventually I put out a few paragraphs. I told it exactly as I saw it, and the quotes were used late last night in a briefing requested by the media. Eventually got to bed, didn't sleep and then got up and did the regular Sunday morning press conference. I thought it very important that I attend to back up the words that I had put out in the statement last night and to show clearly that it was me speaking and I was happy to take questions on the issue. I wanted things to be transparent and out in the open. The New Zealand press put a big spin on it – special press conference called by the Lions to discuss the Umaga incident, etc. As every single NZ journalist who has covered this tour knows full well, Clive does a 'catch-up' press conference early every Sunday morning for the Sunday papers going to bed back at home. If they want to twist the facts into something different, then that's up to them. But let's make sure the facts are recorded here for posterity.

The 'best' TV pictures of the incident were shown on the breakfast-time news this morning in New Zealand – and Saturday evening news back home – and judging by the barrage of texts and calls now arriving they shocked a fair few people, including a number of New Zealanders I know. I went to the 9 a.m. press conference and simply backed up the comments I issued overnight. I am determined to oppose the idea that this is a normal run–of–play, rough–and–tumble injury. It isn't and it needs to be treated differently. I have never complained, publicly, about any injury or incident or cheap shot on me, but this needs to be got out in the open.

Still not a word from Tana. We played back the post-match press conference, and the silence was deafening when Tana was asked about the incident and whether he was disappointed for me. He said sheepishly that there were a couple of incidents that needed looking at. That was his one comment. Graham Henry, the New Zealand coach, expressed ignorance of any incident involving me but said I was a good bloke and it was disappointing if my tour was over.

Monday 27 June, Wellington

Can't sleep with the discomfort, so went down to the team room to look at the match video again. We were very poor, except for defensively, where the boys did very well. Our line-out was all over the place. Just no set-piece possession. Life was going to be hard enough anyway, but you just can't compete if you lose eleven of your own throws. Our decision to change our line-out calls came back to haunt us. It gifted them Ali Williams's try. With no set-piece there was nothing happening behind the scrum and we rarely threatened. My departure and that of Richard Hill definitely unsettled us but didn't affect the result of the game. Given the weather, the All Blacks were excellent. That's the most controlled performance I have ever seen from their pack – they outplayed us and were very disciplined. They didn't give Jonny any chance to keep us in touch and apply pressure with his goal-kicking. Their handling behind the scrum was better than ours, and Tana threw a superb floated pass to make Sivivatu's try, which was absolutely top drawer. One on one Josh Lewsey is as good a defender as there is, but he was shredded by Sivivatu.

Still feeling cheated and violated. The New Zealand papers are reeling off the All Black party line: that there was no foul play and that Tana Umaga had apologized at the press conference. He did no such thing, as everybody knows. He was probably told to say nothing because, as a senior member of the NZRFU media team had admitted privately, they were expecting a citing and didn't want to give our QC, Richard Smith, any ammunition to work with. Apparently Umaga has also been in touch to apologize personally. Again, he has done no such thing. Somebody from the NZRFU has been in touch asking for my cellphone number. Our hotels are in the same part of town: it wouldn't be out of his way to nip over for five minutes or to meet up somewhere near by. As for Mealamu, his part in the incident seems to have been airbrushed out of the proceedings – but not by me.

Digesting the medical news. I need a pinning operation to ensure the ligaments tighten properly and this injury doesn't recur. It is going to be touch and go whether I can get back in time for the autumn internationals – we start against the All Blacks at Lansdowne Road. I will move heaven and earth to make that game – unfinished business you could say – but if the shoulder is not right I will sit it out. I am not going to let this injury be the one that blights my career. I plan on being around for another five or six years at least. I have been pretty lucky so far: torn hamstrings and groins, but nothing major like this.

Forgot to mention that Danny Grewcock got two months for biting, though the judicial finding itself states that Keven Mealamu admitted to 'inadvertently' putting his finger in Danny's mouth. I've played rugby since mini days and I can't remember a single incident of any player in any game 'inadvertently' putting a finger in somebody's mouth. Mentioned it to Dad, and he couldn't think of a similar incident either. Biting is a very serious issue, and if Danny was guilty he deserves everything the authorities dish out, but I have not seen a single shred of evidence against him yet. The video clip of Mealamu complaining about a toothmark on his hand is not even remotely enough to base a citing on, let alone deprive a player of his livelihood. The only evidence appears to be the testimony of two New Zealand players. When it comes to Danny they are being allowed to have their say, but when it comes to me nobody is allowed to utter a word.

Watched the news this evening – very little on any channel except the Umaga incident. One of the NZ stations interviewed Andrew Cole back in Australia. Apparently he doesn't remember coming on to the pitch or seeing anything or telling Umaga and Mealamu to put me down. Curious case of amnesia from somebody who was shouting at them quite audibly. And having come out with that, he then clammed up and told the New Zealand interviewer that he shouldn't really say anything. I think he said exactly what he wanted to say. Disturbing to think he is refereeing the second Test on Saturday, but we daren't say a word or else we will be accused of bringing undue pressure on the referee. There was a revealing moment in another item when they panned around the Basin Reserve cricket ground, where the All Blacks were training. The camera lingered for a moment on a woman and her two kids, who were dressed up in All Blacks garb. The woman was holding a placard: 'Shame Tana – Cheap Shot'.

Tuesday 28 June, Wellington

Graham Henry was challenged three times today on his assertion that Tana had apologized after the game. He stuck to his guns . . . until the NZRFU checked the tapes and then admitted – privately, of course – that they were mistaken. All Blacks can never be wrong and certainly can never apologize in public. Graham was clearly talking nonsense, and I am surprised and disappointed, having worked so closely with him four years ago. Apparently the All Blacks are briefing journalists privately that Graham apologized on Tana's behalf. How mad is this? The Lions stand accused of spinning a story – if you believed some, nothing happened at all and I am walking around with my arm in a sling munching painkillers and anti-inflammatories for fun – and all the time it is the Kiwis who are trying to play with people's minds and muddy the waters so that the truth never really comes out.

All these accusations of Lions spin are missing the point. The Lions played bloody poorly on Saturday and deserved a slating – I know that we have been copping it 24/7 since Saturday evening back home and to an extent rightly so. But does that make it 'spinning' if there is actually an incident that needs covering as well? I seem to remember Graham Henry once spent a couple of years trying to convince the world Shane Howarth and Brett Sinkinson were Welsh before it turned out that they were ineligible and the two New Zealanders were chucked out of international rugby. I don't think we need to take lectures from Graham in particular and New Zealanders in general about spin and misinterpreting facts.

Was having a coffee in the hotel this morning when a clearly sympathetic New Zealander just came up and almost ordered me to read today's *New Zealand Herald* editorial. He didn't want to elaborate, just urged me to read the editorial – not territory I would normally cover. That was this morning, and I have only just got my hands on a copy in the ninth-floor executive coffee and business lounge of the Inter-Continental, which looks out over the harbour. The *Herald* is New Zealand's national paper, but it is printed in Auckland, and editions don't seem to get down here until the afternoon. Here are the relevant passages about the tackle:

'It was, at the very least, a reckless and dangerous act. As such it was unbecoming of a man [Tana Umaga] who won plaudits for stopping play to tend to the unconscious Wales captain Colin Charvis during a Test in Hamilton. It may even have been malicious.

'O'Driscoll's anger seemed directed as much at the All Blacks' reaction as the tackle itself. Quite reasonably he suggested it should have been a matter of "common courtesy" for Umaga to check the condition of the opposing captain before he was taken by stretcher from the field. It is indeed unfathomable that a player of the All Blacks' captain's reputation did not extend that courtesy.

'The Lions captain also suggested that Umaga's lack of action may have been influenced by a sense of guilt. If there was an element of mischief in that there may also be a snippet of truth. Certainly Umaga was, again, not keen to traverse the incident at the post-match press conference.

'His cause was not helped by the like-minded attitude of

the All Black management. The coaches must have recognized the enormity of the incident. They should have come to the press conference willing to talk about it from an All Black perspective.

'The Lions also have an obvious cause for grievance over the curious workings of the citing commissioner Willem Venter, who decided that video evidence of the incident was inconclusive and then flew out of Christchurch on Sunday morning. Clearly the Lions and rugby followers deserved a fuller explanation of why Umaga and Mealamu were not cited. And why Venter could leave the country so quickly?

'Touchjudge Andrew Cole's part in the affair was also odd. He appeared ready to draw the tackle to the referee's attention but then opted not to. Perhaps, ironically, he was influenced by the distaste of the Lions coach for intervention from the sideline.

'Two Tests remain in this series. As always they will be examinations of character and sportsmanship as well as of rugby prowess. It is now especially important for the good name of New Zealand rugby that the All Blacks pass all those tests.'

Bloody hell. Eureka. Make up your own minds, but that is as fair and as objective a look at the entire incident as we are ever likely to get. I am going to tuck it away safely somewhere. When this complete bloody nightmare recedes I will bring it out occasionally. It cuts through the acres of bullshit beautifully and will remind me that I wasn't going mad.

Just back from Palmerston North, where the boys responded well after the disappointment of last Saturday with a record 109–6 win over the local second division club. Seventeen tries, with five for Shane Williams, which will see him claim a Test spot on Saturday. Donncha O'Callaghan will probably get the nod as well after another good performance, and Jason Robinson also looked a bit more like his old self.

The Lions crowd showed a lot of solidarity. There were T-shirts with 'wanted' pictures of Tana Umaga and another which read 'Keven Mealamu, Tana Umaga and Michael Jackson all innocent. Yeah, right.'

Just received a voicemail message: 'Tana here, phone me.' No I'm not the most comfortable at leaving voice messages myself – anybody can feel awkward and be a little abrupt – but it falls some way short of the fulsome apology and expression of concern that the New Zealand camp were proclaiming earlier today.

Still puzzled by his behaviour. I always believed it was he, among the truly hard men of the world game, who never crossed the line, but he was a bitter disappointment on this occasion. Watch the video and you can see a trip on Jason Robinson, a forearm smash into Jonny Wilkinson's face and a very questionable tackle on Josh Lewsey. It was a highly charged occasion, and I daresay if you had a dedicated camera on other players – Lions and All Blacks – you would see things that might warrant investigation. But that does not excuse anything. Everybody has to be accountable for their own actions, on and off the field. I like to think it was an aberration – but it needs to be owned up to.

The entire incident left me sick to the bone for a couple of days before I got myself back together. Dad is brilliant when the going is tough, and he simply stated time and time again that I was lucky not to have had my neck broken and let's just celebrate the fact that I was alive and well. I will forgive but I will never forget how I have been treated over this affair. I've shifted everything to a small corner of my mind and I am already beginning to move on and plot my recovery. The bottom line is that I have a badly dislocated shoulder, it's a rugby injury, it happens and I have got to get back because I am far from finished. But I have learned some very painful lessons about trust and respect and how completely ruthless the All Blacks can be when they want something. I am not going to change my attitudes, though, I am not going to act like that.

And finally something that has put everything into perspective: a text from a friend back in Dublin, who was a good player at Belvedere College. At seventeen he broke his neck playing rugby and is a quadriplegic. 'Both of us have many things in common. Same birthdays, both stunners, both great rugby players! and we have both taken personal setbacks with honour and dignity. Despite your recent hurt you remain a Living Lion legend, Donal O'Flynn.'

Wednesday 29 June, Inter-Continental Hotel

Can't sleep at all with this bloody arm and, having popped myself full of sleepers, I then feel groggy as hell in the morning. The hangover from hell without the fun of having had a drink. Logged in to the internet earlier, trying to keep occupied. Gradually began to realize how the Umaga incident has been dominating the sports pages and chatrooms. Just downloaded a few comments from the *Sunday Telegraph* site. I'm becoming mellow about it now, the anger has subsided massively since receiving Donal's message. I read the comments as if they were about somebody else and they didn't concern me at all.

Have just watched the All Blacks team announcement, with Tana being grilled by the press. Still didn't say much – 'sorry' seems to be the hardest word – but it was Keven Mealamu laughing and grinning throughout in the background who attracted my attention. Don't quite understand why everything is so uproariously funny.

If Tana phones me today I will give him the time of day. I won't let him off the hook completely, but I will hear him out and keep my cool. Like Donal said, you have to face setbacks with honour and dignity. I like to think that perhaps he is not entirely happy with the way things have been handled and feels boxed into a corner.

Thursday 30 June, Inter-Continental Hotel

Woke up this morning with the 'incident' cleared in my head, although I expect it will rumble on a little. I decided not to go to an official reception at the Parliament building – the so-called Beehive – in Wellington last night, where Tana and I had long been booked in for a photo-shoot. Firstly, I wasn't feeling that great; secondly, it took no imagination to predict that it could have turned into a media zoo, with everybody wanting pictures of 'the handshake'. That's not the way I want to resolve this issue.

Later last night Tana finally rang: 'Sorry you got hurt,' he said. We then said a couple of things that will for ever remain private and finished by agreeing to bury the hatchet. I've always made clear my admiration for everything that Tana stands for in rugby and am going to treat the incident as an aberration. Going over my entries for the last three or four days there is no disguising my anger and disappointment, but there comes a point when, instead of just talking about moving on, you have to do something to make that happen. Donal O'Flynn's text message was the key moment for me in that process, plus my own belief that nothing that happens on a rugby pitch should ever affect a personal friendship.

So as of today – Thursday 30 June – I have officially moved on.

Glenda is coming over tomorrow, which is great. I hadn't wanted her around when I was an active participant in the Tests, but her arrival now can't come quickly enough. She was fantastic about the original decision and now here she is rushing around the world when it's all gone pear-shaped for me. It has been a real jolt – not quite sure that is the right word – to realize exactly how much you rely on family and loved ones. After all my nerves and doubts leading into the first Test – with the feeling this was something I had to go through on my own and my efforts to distance myself a little from people – it was fantastic, and very humbling, to realize just how great it was to have my two sisters and Tomás with me on the night before the game. It was exactly what the doctor ordered.

You will have to take my word for this: I was feeling fantastic when I ran out at the Jade Stadium last Saturday night, just perfectly cooked. Relaxed and alert. And then, in the immediate aftermath, having Mum and Dad around has been very reassuring. And now Glenda is on her way. I might have to revise my views on letting people get close to me in the build-up to big matches. There has to be a happy medium.

Apparently Eddie O'Sullivan fired off this afternoon over the Umaga incident. I don't blame him – he has been my national coach for five years and was upset and emotional about everything and is more entitled than most to have his say when asked – but I have now put it to one side and suggest others do likewise. We have to try and do some of our talking on the pitch. It's an awesome task – the All Blacks were good last week but will get significantly better on Saturday. We must somehow raise our game. Training has been sharp this week and 'Alfie' Thomas – my replacement as captain – has been inspirational in restoring morale, but we are definitely up against it.

Had a stroll – not a 'relaxing stroll', a normal stroll – around Wellington this afternoon, and the Lions fans are still 100 per cent supportive. The weather has been fabulous – clear skies and blazing sun, which is unusual for Wellington in the winter – and the majority appear to be having the time of their lives. Their enthusiasm is infectious. The first Test went badly wrong, but apart from that this has been a happy tour, and the fans have had a ball. Not everything is doom and gloom.

Prince William has arrived in New Zealand and called in to the team hotel. He is a nice lad – what am I saying, I'm only three years older myself – and very grounded. I've met him once before – we had a good chat at a reception in Cardiff before the Argentina game. He got his wires a bit crossed and asked Andy Robinson if he was coming down to New Zealand at all to watch the series in New Zealand.

'Bad luck, old mate,' were William's opening words to me down in the hotel lobby a few minutes ago. Some of the lads have taken him off to a café to fill him in on the tour to date. Hopefully we will get a few beers inside him before the weekend is over.

Just took a call from a very eminent former Irish Lion whom I respect immensely on and off the field. He sympathized totally with my injury and the circumstances surrounding it and said the New Zealanders had acted very poorly and evaded the real issue. But he also said that the 'incident' had to end because it was overshadowing the tour, and that can never be allowed to happen. I thanked him, genuinely, and said that I agreed absolutely and that I had already come to exactly the same conclusion some time ago. Quite how you end it is another matter. Except for a short sit-down briefing with the Irish journalists on Tuesday for the tour debrief piece they badly needed from me to fill their pages back home, I haven't uttered a public word since the Sunday-morning press conference, when I thought it vital to back up my anonymous press statement words of the night before with a public appearance. But it flared up at the New Zealand public day on Monday and both the All Black press conferences on Tuesday and Wednesday. I can't stop people asking questions. People keep on throwing fuel on to the fire.

Friday 1 July, Inter-Continental Hotel

Fell off the wagon a little bit last night and treated myself to a fair few consolation beers – well, it had to come after all the emotion of the last week. Actually it was in very pleasant circumstances – I found myself in the company of some of the All Blacks, Conrad Smith, Doug Howlett and James Ryan, who aren't involved in the match tomorrow and were enjoying a rare run ashore themselves. They were excellent company, with Conrad a particularly engaging and bright guy, a trainee lawyer no less. From what I saw of him on the Blacks' autumn tour he is some player as well. New Zealand have incredible strength in depth in some positions, centre being one of them. Ma'a Nonu is another very useful operator who hasn't made a start yet.

Yet another gorgeous day and just counting the hours until Glenda arrives. I have managed to keep going, just, this week by busying myself with the team, going to training and attending all the meetings, but that only takes you so far. The bottom line is that I am now a non-playing captain and with the second Test upon us I am feeling very much on the sidelines. Trying hard not to feel sorry for myself, but it's difficult.

Saturday 2 July, Inter-Continental Hotel

We are off to the Westpac Stadium in an hour's time, the moment of truth as far as the 2005 Lions tour is concerned. After months of build-up everything has happened very quickly. It could all be over tonight – eight days and the series gone. Got my fingers crossed for this evening – sides have won in such circumstances – but we will need to produce something very special.

Felt very relaxed this morning with Glenda here and helping to take the strain. She knows how disappointed I am deep down but says all the right things, and of course with her here the rugby doesn't seem quite so all-important. We had a huge family gathering and meal last night, which was the social highlight of the tour to date and has seen me wake up this morning in very good form. Growing to really love Wellington, exploring all its streets and little cafés. The winter sun is still beating down and there are some huge waves down on the beaches. It's probably the one place in New Zealand where I could happily settle and live.

Everywhere you look some of the Lions supporters' 1800 campervans seem to be parked up, and the hotel is mobbed downstairs. Brilliant pre-match buzz – reminds me of some of Ireland's World Cup games down in Australia. Kiwis tell me they have never seen anything like this. The Lions have brought something very special to New Zealand.

Just read a nice line in one of the New Zealand papers from Colin Meads: 'Tana should have been around the Lions team hotel on Saturday night, Sunday night at the latest, with a crate of beer. It might have been frosty to start, but the thaw would have soon started. There is a lot of merit in the old ways.'

Yes, it would have been very, very frosty – arctic even – but yes, Colin Meads is right, it would almost certainly have thawed!

Sunday 3 July, Hilton Hotel, Auckland

That's it, we've lost the series. Our dreams and hard work have amounted to absolutely nothing. Felt pretty empty and useless when I woke up this morning and am thinking of home for the first time. There is nothing I can contribute to this tour any more, but I have got to keep going for another seven or eight days. All the lads will be feeling down, and I must try to stay upbeat.

We got beaten 48–18 last night by an awesome All Blacks side. The funny thing is we played infinitely better than last week. The scoreline was cruel – New Zealand were probably fifteen points better on the night – but some days the scoreline can get away from you a little. You don't take your chances and they capitalize on all of theirs. There was no disgrace at all, but the better side definitely won.

We couldn't have made a better start, Gareth Thomas

taking his second-minute try with real panache. And then Jonny had a penalty that could have made it 10–0; he hit the post, Jason Robinson regathered, and we were odds on to get a penalty or drop a goal or even score a second try when a pumped-up Paul O'Connell went flying into a ruck and gave away a penalty. These were important moments, you have to take every single opportunity when you play New Zealand. Dan Carter kicked a penalty and Tana Umaga scored a breakaway try after we spilled good possession in midfield. Even then we should have stopped the counter-attack at source but missed a couple of tackles. We could have been 14–3 up but soon found ourselves 13–7 down. Very frustrating. Tana's try certainly got the crowd going, the New Zealand section of it anyway. He had been loudly booed by the Lions supporters when his name had been read out before the kick-off. I can imagine exactly how sweet he must have felt touching down.

New Zealand struck decisively, but slightly fortuitously, just before the break with a breath-taking team try, finished off by Sitiveni Sivivatu after sensational handling by the backs. I say fortuitously because the Blacks had been mysteriously given the scrum on our line when Byron Kelleher clung on to the ball for ever as they pressed our line and he went to ground. He would still be clutching it for dear life now if Andrew Cole hadn't pulled play up and inexplicably given the Blacks the put-in as opposed to a penalty to the Lions. You can look at that passage of play 100 times on the video and every time it is a penalty to the Lions. No question. But on this occasion, completely randomly, the decision goes against us. These are the little individual moments which help shape a game. Having said that, the Blacks' handling to create the try, especially out of the tackle, was sensational – way ahead of anything in Britain and Ireland at the moment. Sometimes it is more basketball and handball than rugby, and I know they start most of their training sessions with a hybrid game of Aussie Rules, Gaelic football and basketball, passing the ball in any direction. It clearly helps their hand–eye coordination and passing skills and perhaps we should be doing something similar.

After the break we had to score first to keep in the game, but New Zealand were well aware of that and upped their game massively to produce forty minutes of supreme rugby, orchestrated by Carter, who kicked all his goals and scored two sumptuous tries. I have never seen a better individual performance at international level. He has got everything: handling skills, kicking ability out of hand and at goal, and serious pace. He wouldn't look out of place on the wing and had played centre in Test rugby before. The local paper gave him eleven out of ten this morning in their player ratings. Fair enough! We kept going, with our pack – unlike last week – delivering a steady stream of set-piece possession. Steve Thompson was back to his best, making his presence felt and throwing well. Simon Easterby capped a superb individual performance with a try, and we should have scored at least one more but somehow managed not to rumble the ball over from a series of line-outs on their line.

No complaints, though. Carter's brace of tries were brilliantly executed and Richie McCaw capped yet another memorable display at openside by forcing his way over. What a player he is, a real warrior. Hard as nails but completely fair and legit. I reckon he wasn't far off eleven out of ten either! New Zealand were worthy winners, and I doubt if many sides in Lions history could have lived with them. You can rehearse all the arguments you want about this tour, but how many Lions sides in history have faced a side quite this good?

You could do nothing other than stand back and applaud the All Blacks, which is exactly what we did, going into their changing room. There was a good atmosphere, all the tension and misunderstandings of earlier in the week disappearing. Clive congratulated them – genuinely and generously, in my opinion – and then stepped out to face the critics who were sharpening their pencils in the press room. He has endured a very tough week and he looked very tired and appeared quite emotional.

The lads are battered but nowhere near as down as last week, they know they gave a much better and more honest account of themselves. More injuries, though. Jonny has picked up a painful stinger on his shoulder again after trying to tackle Tana Umaga and falling awkwardly diving at Dan Carter. He is very unlikely to play again on this tour. Gavin Henson is also struggling with a stinger which has left him numb, so we have got real problems in midfield again. Ironic. Arriving here, it was one of the positions where I felt we had real strength in depth, and yet it has been a problem almost from the start.

Prince William came into the dressing room to commiserate, and I take my hat off to him for that. A dressing room can be a pretty volatile place after a big defeat, and he could have been excused for making himself scarce, but he handled it just right. At one point I just said, 'Howaya, Willie,' and he sat down on the bench with me and we chatted about the game for ten minutes, both feeling a little bit out of it in our own ways. Prince 'Willie' indeed – I know I am going to get stick about that, but it seemed the natural thing to say, and he didn't bat an eyelid.

Not in the mood to analyse the tour in any great detail at

the moment, though obviously all the media have declared their instant verdict, which is not very flattering. Anyway there are two matches to go yet, and there will be plenty of time in the coming week to think it through. The one thing that haunts me already, though, is the question of how could we be so well prepared and such a happy bunch together and yet fall so short? For whatever reason, the X factor, the spark, wasn't there when we needed it. Why was that? We have good players and generally we trained very well. My gut instinct is that we are not far from clicking and if we started the series again tomorrow on the back of our five weeks here we would go very close indeed. We were definitely a week short of being 'good to go', to use one of Eddie's favourite expressions. Perhaps there is a minimum stretch of time – five weeks? – that a Lions team needs touring in the southern hemisphere before you can expect it to happen. It takes time and patience for everything to come together at club and provincial level, so why should it be different at international level? Anyway, I will save the real soul-searching for next week sometime.

Enjoyed a late one last night, with many of the Blacks and Lions hitting the town together. I caught Justin Marshall's eye at one point and immediately went up to the bar to shake his hand. I was going to say something embarrassing and maybe a little crass re his much-appreciated gesture in Christchurch, but something inside me said now wasn't the time and place – in public with the two sides finally enjoying a relaxed evening together. It might ignite things again. So instead we just chatted for ages about rugby and his move to Leeds in a couple of weeks. Justin was superb in the opening Test, and terrific again last night as a replacement. His service is unbelievable and unless my eyes deceive me he seems to be getting quicker and fitter around the pitch as he gets older. One of the great All Blacks and still in his pomp. People seem to be retiring him, but it takes no leap of the imagination to see him back in the New Zealand mix come the 2007 World Cup if Byron Kelleher gets injured or loses form and nobody else comes through at scrum-half.

Justin has got the golf bug bad. I told him to give me a ring if he fancied a short golfing break in Ireland, I would arrange everything. He sounded very enthusiastic and muttered something about looking out for his old mate Andrew Mehrtens, who will be over with Harlequins and keen to improve his already impressive handicap of two. One way or another those two are going to be great signings for their clubs, and I suspect they will have a lot of fun along the way.

Took the opportunity to go down to a final press briefing tonight, which surprised all the scribes, who were expecting just a quiet chat with one or two of the lads. I don't want to be involved in an official front this coming week so I wanted to get any outstanding issues dealt with there and then. Tried to explain to them how mystifying it was that we just didn't click, but what a huge ask it was always going to be to build a team in six weeks to defeat the All Blacks on their own turf. Taking my cue from the very eminent Irish former Lion, I wasn't going to raise the Tana issue in any shape or form, but of course the question eventually came, so I just played a completely straight bat. We had made our peace, everybody concerned has moved on and I look forward to enjoying a pint with Tana at some stage. He is a great player and had been on the top of his form during this season. His displays in the Test series have been superb.

Monday 4 July, Hilton Hotel

Horrible, miserable, grey, rainy day in Auckland. The sense of anti-climax is almost suffocating and nothing seems fun any more. That includes the Hilton Hotel, stuck down here on the wharf; it doesn't seem like 'home' any more, as I remember writing a while back, when the weather was bright and sunny and we were full of hope. Now the place feels like a prison. I can be very fickle! Frankly, I can't get home quick enough. God knows what the boys who have to play again this week are feeling.

Can't even summon the energy to visit the casino and recoup a few losses on the poker table. I'm not really needed here and I feel like a hanger-on. It's odd, though, because I don't feel like I deserve a holiday either. Just forty seconds of Test rugby, that has been my sole contribution. I feel a fraud taking the tour payment and want to hit the gym and train like a maniac to put things right, but I can't even do that until the operation and the proper rehab.

I'm also a bit anxious. I've had various soft tissue injuries in the past, but this is the first time my body has been really damaged, and these shoulder injuries can come back to haunt you – think of the agonies people like Keith Wood went through. I need the operation in Dublin next week to go perfectly and the rehab to be trouble free. If that happens it's onwards and upwards. If there are any problems it could be a long haul.

It's probably not the best day to record random thoughts, because my mood is matching the crap weather, but I've got some time on my hands and a couple of themes keep forcing themselves into my mind.

I don't like New Zealand anywhere near as much as I did three years ago when I visited with Ireland. I exclude Wellington from that comment – I felt a real buzz about the place and would like to experience more. That may sound a bit odd, considering it was such a difficult week there for me, but I immediately felt at home. The rest of New Zealand has left me with very mixed feelings. There is a real edge to the supporters and man in the street that I don't remember at all from my previous visit – some pretty nasty abuse from fans and loutish and boorish behaviour when you are out and about in a café or pub. I read that after the Christchurch Test there were twenty-two arrests, and every single arrest had been a New Zealander for drunken or violent behaviour. Not one Lions fan stepped out of line, despite the oceans of beer they consumed. I am proud of the Lions supporters and, at the same time, not overly surprised at the statistic about the New Zealand fans.

Having been here six weeks now I would also say that their obsession with rugby borders on the unhealthy. Being passionate about something is fine, but rugby dominates too much down here, to the exclusion of everything else. Rugby is too important and their obsession results in tunnel vision. There has to be a life outside of rugby, especially in such a gorgeous country with everything going for it.

There are exceptions, of course – I have met some great Kiwis and thoroughly enjoyed shooting the breeze with some of the All Blacks – but generally I have found it hard going. Perhaps I have been hemmed in by the captaincy, which has made it harder to be myself, but I don't think so. As for their press, I just can't read the stuff they print some days. It's completely unplayable. One-eyed is being much too kind. They report on completely different games to the one I have witnessed or played in. They make mountains out of molehills of any alleged Lions indiscretion and virtually ignore any from their own side. It's very curious, because the average Kiwi fan has a deep knowledge of the game and can quickly appreciate exactly what happened for themselves. The majority of New Zealand fans who spoke to me after the Umaga incident acknowledge that 'something' had definitely happened and not been dealt with properly; but their press, with the honourable exception of the *Herald* leader, seemed out of step with public sentiment.

It would be much healthier, surely, if New Zealand had another couple of major sports to share the headlines – rugby would have to compete for space and the reporting would have to be more critical.

Have just been reading a few comments from JPR Williams which made me laugh out loud at first and then think seriously about what lay behind them. JPR was quoted as saying that 'The problem with the 2005 Lions is that they didn't sleep together!' Reading on, JPR was really making the point that in the old days, sharing rooms with a player from another country, experiencing the rough and tumble of regular Saturday–Wednesday rugby and travelling around the country together by train and old planes helped form a really tight squad. I would not dismiss what he says. You can definitely become stronger and closer in adversity – rugby is full of stories of backs-to-the-wall performances against the odds by close-knit sides. But I don't think you can set out in the modern era to deliberately make things tough for the players. Slotting in a Lions tour is not easy in the professional age. If you make the tour too spartan, players won't tour. They are already coming off the back of an exhausting nine-month season, and unlike old Lions tourists they have to start back at their clubs late in July. Gareth Edwards used to delay his debut for Cardiff until mid–October after a Lions tour. In the amateur days that was the player's prerogative. Somewhere in the middle is the happy medium. There is undoubtedly a science to this touring business, and getting it absolutely right is the trick to being successful.

Trying to be smiley and positive if I bump into any of the midweek side to play Auckland tomorrow night. This is going to be a very difficult week, and it's important we keep our heads held high. Having said that, the Midweek Massive, as they have termed themselves, need little motivation to preserve their unbeaten record on tour. This is their big moment now, and I fancy the motivation will come from within.

For all our intention not to split the squad into separate Saturday and midweek set-ups, the truth is that on a Lions tour you cannot avoid having a midweek side, and ultimately you cannot slide out of labelling them. It's how you treat them that really counts, and we did that very well on this tour. They were given one of the best coaches in the world – Ian McGeechan – to concentrate totally on their needs, with the excellent back-up of Gareth 'Paaaaashuun' Jenkins and Ireland's defensive man Mike Ford, who has enjoyed a fine tour. The lads have been given a full six or seven days lead-in time to prepare for every game and offered every facility. Ultimately their performances have counted: witness the raft of changes we made after the first Test with players being drafted in from the Massive. They could not have received more back-up had they been in the Test team and they have quickly formed their own identity, mainly under the captaincy of Gordon Bulloch and Michael Owen, who have done excellent jobs.

There has probably never been an itinerary like it for the midweekers. Monday-night game against Argentina in Cardiff, Wednesday-night game against Taranaki in New Plymouth, Saturday[!] game against Otago in Dunedin, flying Tuesday-night visit to Southland, Tuesday-night game against Manawatu and now finally their 'Test' against Auckland in front of 47,000 fans at Eden Park.

Tuesday 5 July, Hilton Hotel

Feeling much chirpier this morning after an enjoyable visit to the Starship Children's Hospital in Auckland with my new best friend Willie – Prince William to you! – and Andrew Sheridan, whose ankle has flared up again and forced him to drop out of tonight's game. You can't mooch around feeling down for too long when you see such brave kids fighting illness – and I must say in all honesty I have enjoyed all our hospital visits on this tour. I was a little nervous beforehand, but they have been a highlight. William is a complete natural with young people, just like his mother, and the entire morning went with a swing and had a feelgood air about it. Very uplifting.

Wonder what Willie is doing at this precise moment. I only say that because while on the hospital visit I delivered a very official and important-looking letter to him in a brown envelope from my cousin Gary, who is emerging as one of the tour's big pranksters and jokers. Inside the envelope was a spoof Midweek Massive application form, inviting William to sign on the dotted line and join the week of celebration that will follow tonight's game. You know the kind of thing: Favourite drink? Personal best on number of beers consumed?

Preferred method of payment for bar bill? Can you sing? Favourite song when called upon? Have you ever streaked? Blondes or brunettes? And so on. Hopefully he will fill it out and join the lads on the session, though I'm pretty sure he told me he was off on a skiing trip to Queenstown and some official visits in Christchurch before coming back to Auckland.

Weather is still horrible but have been out and about town this afternoon with Glenda and am just enjoying a cuppa before tonight's game. Hope we can produce something good tonight, for the fans as much as ourselves. Auckland is swarming with supporters in red shirts and Lions anoraks, all soaked to the skin in the rain and looking pretty sorry and downcast. It must be very hard for them, saving up maybe for years for the two- or three-week visit of a lifetime, and now such a downbeat week with the series gone, and the rain lashing down in murky Auckland. More than any other city I know, Auckland needs the sun to bring it alive. My heart goes out to the fans and I feel horribly responsible for everything, not that there is a single thing I can do except smile for photos whenever I am asked and generally pass the time of day and thank them genuinely for all their support. It would be brilliant if we could get a win tonight and at least put a smile on their faces so they can enjoy their beer for the rest of the week and feel like partying with the Kiwis.

Auckland are fielding virtually their Super 12 team – they haven't enjoyed the best of Super 12 seasons but they will play as a unit and will probably be the strongest provincial opposition we'll have encountered on tour. I have confidence in the Midweek Massive; they have real character and have trained really hard for the last three or four days. There are a few players who could still play themselves into the Test team – Charlie Hodgson or ROG (with Jonny out injured), Geordan Murphy, Gordon D'Arcy, who looked close to his best against Manawatu, Simon Shaw and Mark Cueto. Others, like Gordon Bulloch and Graham Rowntree, will probably think they are making their last appearance in a Lions shirt and will be very keen to finish on a high note.

Wednesday 6 July, Hilton Hotel

Top effort from the lads, a gutsy 17–13 win over Auckland and a smile again on everybody's face. Very pleased for all concerned, especially Ian McGeechan, whose last match it might be as a Lions coach – though I wouldn't be surprised to see him pop up again in South Africa in four years' time – and captain Gordon Bulloch, who has done a brilliant job keeping the boys together.

After all the rain the ball was very slippery, and the game wasn't a classic, but it was very feisty and competitive – to say the least – and we were good value for the win. At one stage, going into half-time 14–3, I thought we were going to pull away in style, but, as we have discovered to our cost, if you don't put these Kiwi sides away when you get the opportunity they come snapping back at you.

We started very smoothly, with Charlie Hodgson showing definite Test-match class before he got concussed going back bravely to fall on a loose ball after Denis Hickie had a kick ahead charged down. It's funny how some people get labelled. Charlie apparently is 'weak defensively'. What rubbish. I can remember just one missed tackle from him all tour, and even that is probably a harsh call: he was trying to defend a two-on-one when Otago scored their first-half try in

Dunedin. Even then he managed to slow their centre down. Charlie on this tour has been close to the top of the tackle counts in all his games.

We went into half-time on a high after brilliant work from Mark Cueto led to a try for Martyn Williams in the corner. Mark allowed a loose pass to bounce up and effectively used the bounce to dummy the defender before setting off on a 50-yard run, sidestepping a couple of defenders. At one point I thought he would get across for the try of the tour but he got hauled down a yard short, and Matt Dawson quickly recycled for Martyn to score. Terrific work and just the high point of a stunning display which also included a couple of memorable defensive clearances.

Mark has been unlucky on this tour, with limited opportunities to show his talent. I felt when he joined us following Iain Balshaw's withdrawal that he would challenge for a Test place. He certainly put his hand up last night, but I would still be surprised if Shaggy didn't get the nod on Saturday.

It was a pretty physical match. Ben Kay was rabbit-punched in the eye when he was trying to get the ball off Sam Tuitupou after Auckland had been penalized in front of their posts, and Tuitupou blatantly and illegally walked off with the ball, preventing us taking a quick penalty. It should probably have been a penalty try anyway because Martyn Williams was tackled before he had the ball with the line beckoning. Ben just tried to strip Tuitupou of the ball and got smacked for his troubles, a nasty black eye that closed immediately and forced him off. In the end it was us who got penalized, but then Steve Walsh was the referee. I better not get started on that subject again because I will say something that will land me in trouble.

He and the officials missed another ugly incident in the

second half when our friend Tuitupou tried to scalp Gordon D'Arcy with a nasty kick in the head at a ruck, the ball nowhere near. The crowd were a bit aghast when the replay flashed up on the screen, but officialdom decided to do nothing.

Gordon looked pretty groggy but battled on. Tuitupou, when concentrating on rugby, and young Ben Atiga are dangerous runners, but Darce did really well defensively last night. Glad he has had an upbeat finish to the tour after his earlier problems. He is now back on top form, though he is so battered that he will probably be unavailable for Saturday, which is a shame because he would definitely have been in the mix along with Shaggy and Mark.

So we held on, and the Midweek Massive party began, to which I was invited and partook freely. They did us proud last night and have done themselves proud. Southland was their only poor performance, but I was probably too harsh on them when I wrote about it earlier. They really care about the Lions and will have been devastated at not making the first Test. To turn around less than three days after the Otago game and go again was massively difficult, and to actually come away sneaking a win was all we could ask.

Ian McGeechan has been a true star on this tour. He has obviously enjoyed being back in a tracksuit organizing sessions after his spell as an administrator at the SRU. It has been a regret of mine that I have spent so little time training under him. I thoroughly enjoyed the two or three days' training when he took charge of the prospective Test team for the Wellington game. Everything was done swiftly and with precision, in fact it was nigh-on perfect – we didn't have to backtrack on anything. It wasn't so much a technical thing, it was the atmosphere he set, challenging top-quality players to sort it out themselves and display their skill. The awful weather in Wellington on match night prevented us from showing anything much in the game itself, but we were humming in training that week.

My other regret is that we have trained so little as a squad of forty-five or whatever because it was considered impractical after a fairly chaotic joint session in Auckland during our first week. I believe we needed more sessions together, to foster that feeling of being a complete squad, if nothing else. You could sometimes go nearly a week without seeing some guys if you were busy playing a match somewhere and they were back at base preparing for the next game. I don't know what the answer is, but future tours need to watch out for this.

Another awful day weatherwise, New Zealand really has saved up its worst for last. Can't help thinking back to what I've read concerning the 1977 tour, an old-style three-month affair in which they only had three days when it didn't rain. The famous mud-man pictures of Fran Cotton come from that tour. Weather like that would have driven me mad. The fact that that Lions team swept through the Provinces and only lost the Test series in the final minutes of the fourth Test fills me with renewed respect for that generation.

A lot of battered bodies around, so Clive has cancelled all training for the day and delayed selecting the team for Saturday. Gordon D'Arcy is in bits after his brave effort on Tuesday night and has just told Clive that he is in no state to be considered for Saturday. That is an honest and brave thing to say, because while my preference, on tour form, would be for Shaggy at centre with Gareth Thomas, Darce had played his way into better form. Gareth is down with the flu but is determined to muddle through. New Zealand are also struggling with injuries – Aaron Mauger, Daniel Carter and Richie McCaw are all out.

Just got back into the hotel and there was a lot of excitement from some of the lads gathered around the TV bar. London, against all the odds, has won the vote for the 2012 Olympics. A lot of happy Englishmen with big smiles. And of course lorryloads of sympathy for the French!

Thursday 7 July, Hilton Hotel

Still chucking it down. The Test team has been announced, with a few interesting selections. Geordan Murphy gets the nod at full-back, Josh moves back to the wing and Mark Cueto comes in on the wing, fulfilling my prediction of nearly two months ago that he would finish the tour as a Test player. At centre it's a question of who lines up alongside Gareth, who is determined to play through his flu. Shaggy, most probably, or Will Greenwood? Steve Thompson has been named at hooker but is beginning to cough and splutter badly with the virus that is going around, so Shane Byrne stands by.

Shoulder pain is beginning to ease and I might revert to writing these notes by hand again soon. I am getting lazy and enjoying using the dictaphone, but it will be good physio to start scribbling again. If we left the shoulder alone it would heal up in a fashion, but there is no guarantee whatsoever that it would be strong enough. The surrounding ligaments have been badly torn and stretched and I need them back to perfect strength and alignment to make sure it doesn't pop out again.

Had finished this short entry for the day when I switched

on the TV and saw the terrible news coming out of London about the terrorist bombs scattered around the city at rush hour. Horrible scenes. Went down to the team room where a large group were gathered around the TV. A lot of the lads with friends and family in London have been busy on their mobiles checking in.

Friday 8 July, Hilton Hotel

Completely off tour. I've tried to keep it going but I'm excess baggage now and feeling a long way from home. I'm no use to the 2005 Lions any more, a busted flush. The boys have got to drag themselves through one more match and there is nothing I can do or say that will make it any easier for them. If it was one apiece and everything to play for I could still head the bottle-carriers, cheerleaders and backslappers, but there is no role for me now. Alfie is doing a fantastic job in keeping people going, given the circumstances, and it is time to make myself scarce. Don't intend attending the final team meeting tonight; I must be like a ghost hanging over the bloody place and I feel so down. Don't want any of that communicating itself to the guys. Steve Thompson has withdrawn with the lurgi, so Shane Byrne is back in. I wish the guys every ounce of good luck and will be rooting for them from start to finish tomorrow but I don't feel like I belong any more.

Thank God for Glenda. She has been a star. First of all I mess her around about even coming out at all. Then, when I finally relent, the tour has gone up in smoke and we are marooned in a sodden Auckland with yours truly not in the best of moods. She has been fantastic, a real trouper, and really lifted my spirits. We have been very close this week and I count myself a lucky guy.

We fell into bad company last night with Damo, Ciaran Scally and a few friends. Old mates and a trusted crew. We all went off for a riotous meal. I finally ran up the white flag and admitted, mentally, that my tour was over and kicked back and just enjoyed the banter and a few beers. Good physio for the right arm if nothing else!

And a brilliant warm-up for the big contest, one of the toughest of my career, I suspect. Have agreed to meet Jason Leonard for a couple of 'quiet beers' later tonight, a sure sign of encroaching madness on my part, or the pressing need to let off steam. Jason's 'quiet beers' are legendary. Will report back from the battle front tomorrow morning, but this could get ugly, worse even than facing the All Blacks.

Saturday 9 July, Hilton Hotel

Throbbing hangover, the only one of the tour, which will probably surprise and shock old Lions. Leonard was simply awesome. Judging by his appearance I would say he has been in intensive training for months and has peaked perfectly for the Lions tour. Anyway he blew me away with a world-class performance last night, but then again I am only a lightweight back. Thank God I don't have to drink with him every night, but what marvellous company and what a great pick-me-up for a wounded Lion. Jason has got life in proportion, with nothing – not even humbling defeats against the All Blacks – remotely as important as enjoying the company of mates. Somebody once wrote that 'Every day is Christmas Day in the Leonard household' and they got it exactly right. Feel more than a little ragged this morning but much happier with my lot.

As I've got a full free day on my hands before tonight's kick-off I might as well attempt my tour debrief, or at least my interim thoughts. Clive is going to spend a day with me in Dublin in August, after which he has to submit an official report, but I have some initial thoughts of my own.

Firstly, Clive has copped a heapful of criticism which I consider unwarranted. Would anybody believe me when I say that he has organized this tour brilliantly and it has been one of the best experiences of my life? Ultimately our problem was that we were taking on the impossible, or virtually the impossible. Once in a hundred years the Lions have won a tour in New Zealand, and this is an All Blacks side to rank with the very best.

The idea of bringing forty-five players was completely sound and justified – and I admit I was initially very sceptical. Clive's rationale was misunderstood completely, especially by the Kiwis, who enjoyed mocking the idea. It was purely practical. We knew the attrition rate would be high in New Zealand and to fly replacements in from the UK you basically have to write off a week before they can play. You can travel with streamlined squads if you don't undertake midweek matches, but if you are trying to fulfil an old-fashioned tour, forty-five is now about the correct number. Clive is a radical thinker and perhaps his concept of a Lions tour such as this was too much too soon, but I will be surprised if, in the future, the Lions don't fine-tune most of his ideas.

Like the rest of us he has learned a lot on this tour. It's one thing spectating and commentating on a Lions tour from the sidelines, another thing altogether actually running one. Ironically, after going through the mill over the last couple of months Clive is probably now the ideal man to lead the next Lions tour! In all honesty I would have no qualms whatsoever about touring with Clive again. I would be delighted and honoured and very confident of turning the tables around.

It has also been a very happy tour, with no divisions that I can think of – the occasional sharp word, yes, but nothing more. With more than seventy adults in close confinement for seven weeks, that's remarkable. Lots of laughs and happy times. I don't remember that from four years ago. I have made lifelong friends over the last seven weeks; that didn't really happen in Australia. It's not the reason you go on tour, but it's a massive bonus when it happens.

The night before the first Test I lost the envelope containing all my match tickets for family and friends. A major panic by any standards and exactly what I didn't want. I scarcely had the courage to mention it to Louise Ramsey, our overworked tour manager, but she was incredible. From nowhere she produced a folder with all the numbers of my tickets and was on the phone to the NZRFU ordering replacements. She is obviously well used to dealing with idiot rugby players and disorganized adolescent males. Luckily at that point somebody found the tickets, and she was saved yet another tiresome chore. Louise was extraordinary throughout. She left her home and twelve-month-old baby to look after us for the last two months and nobody could have done it better.

When I am old and grey it will be the 2005 tour I remember rather than the 2001. It was bigger and more intense. Rugby means so much more in New Zealand, the interest has been phenomenal and our supporters absolutely incredible. The nation seemed to stop still for a month or more and the Lions tour was the big story every day.

But we didn't produce on the field. Why? Why? Why? The All Blacks were too good, time was too short and we made a few crucial mistakes. Is that too glib? It was always a very long shot, us winning in New Zealand. It would have been a huge and massive shock, nigh-on a miracle, if we had pulled it off.

The biggest mistake – and I would argue the only core mistake – was not to play the Saturday Test team, or the core of that team, from the outset. The Saturday team were at least one, perhaps two, games short in preparation together. You can make kind noises and use different terminology, but you cannot get away from the old principle of Test team and dirt-trackers. It's just the way it is. I have touched on this before and have now really hardened my thoughts on the subject. It is the only way you can become competitive in such a short time.

The midweek side must get the very best in coaching, and nobody in 2005 can complain in that respect. They must be given every facility and a cast-iron guarantee that if they perform exceptionally well they will be considered for pro-motion. And in turn management must not become precious if some of the dirt-trackers, having given their all in the early games, become a little disillusioned towards the end. That is human nature. We must have the Test team tried, tested and ready to go. If the tour structure is right, the disillusionment among the dirt-trackers will be minimal anyway. The Midweek Massive were a proud bunch and kept it going, only dipping once when they scraped home against South-land. Rather than ease off towards the end of the tour it was a master-stroke to give them their 'Test' – against mighty Auckland – on the final Tuesday. That is a very good pointer to the future, but something you can only really contemplate when travelling with a large squad.

My other observations are of secondary importance, fine tuning if you like. With everybody dashing around New Zealand there were some days when the team preparing for the next game was left short of opposition for contact sessions. I would like to have seen more training sessions together for the entire squad, especially early on. With carefully worked routines we could have done more together.

Selection-wise we all have our own thoughts. I believed in our selection for the first Test, it was working well in training and had the element of just keeping the Kiwis guessing a little, but it clearly didn't work on the night. We have to hold our hands up. It was a gamble and in retrospect we got it wrong, but there was no feeling at all during the week that it was going wrong. Quite the opposite. My memory is that we were buzzing and upbeat and fancied we had a sniff of a chance.

There are good reasons why we lost – a game short in preparation, line-out disaster and the disruption of myself and Richard Hill getting crocked early in the first half – but ultimately it's difficult to legislate against a bad day at the office. It was our big opportunity lost. New Zealand played well in the difficult conditions but were a bit rough around the edges as well, as we thought they might be after a long spell away from international rugby. They were always going to be at their most vulnerable – comparatively speaking, of course – in Christchurch.

I was surprised that Shane Horgan wasn't picked for the second Test and very surprised that he didn't make the starting line-up for the third. He was the stand-out player in training and made an impact every time he came on as a replacement during the tour. Shane has developed into a hard man mentally and physically – he made light of playing with a broken hand against England during the Six Nations – and was itching to get among the Kiwis. He was so up for it and we should have let him loose, probably at inside centre. I was extremely disappointed for him, but it augurs well for Ireland that he has made serious strides on this tour.

I wouldn't take issue with many other selections. Lack of time was the main problem from start to finish. We will never know about the experiment of playing Jonny alongside me at centre because I was off in a trice and we hardly won any usable ball thereafter. All I can say was that I was excited about what we might have achieved and feel frustrated that now we will never know.

It's interesting that two of the tour replacements – Ryan Jones and Simon Easterby – have done as well as anybody on tour, but not really all that strange. Both came within a hair's breadth of making the original party and played like men with points to prove when they finally arrived. Great. That's how it works in sport. There is a well-established tradition of replacement Lions arriving to breathe life into a tour, not least four years ago, when Martin Corry flew from an England tour in Canada and made a terrific impact in the Test side. Martin Johnson flew to New Zealand from an England A tour to Canada in 1993, when Wade Dooley dropped out, and lost no time at all in making the Test spot his own.

Tactically we went into our shells sometimes. In the opening games we worried all the opposition teams with our cross-field kicks – all our fly-halves are expert at it, especially Charlie and ROG. But then we stopped for some reason –

the last one I can remember was Charlie's against Otago, which brought a try for Will Greenwood. No side looked comfortable defending against the cross-field kick.

Sunday 10 July, airborne – somewhere between Sydney and Singapore

Leaving on a jet plane, don't know when I'll be back again. Don't care either for the time being. Just want to get home to Ireland, the best country in the world despite the weather! Long journey ahead and I'm just wishing the hours away.

We got beaten again last night, very similar to the second Test, pretty good, gutsy performance, but flawed as well – and New Zealand were just too good. My new mate Conrad Smith had a terrific match, he looks a very complete player and it will be some competition between him and Aaron Mauger to see who gets the starting spot at inside centre for their big games ahead. The depth New Zealand have in some positions is staggering.

At one stage in the first half we managed to squander a three-man overlap 5 yards from the line. Donncha O'Callaghan went to ground just short of the line, but we should still have scored with men begging on the blindside – except Tana prevented release at the ruck and got a yellow card for his pains. And then, with them down to fourteen men, we let them in for two softish tries. Effectively a twenty-one-point swing in ten minutes. No side in the world can give New Zealand twenty-one points. The match was over there and then, although we kept plugging away gamely. I was proud that our heads never dropped, and there were times up front last night when we began to take control and got those powerful rolling mauls going at last. A hint of what might have been. I would like to have seen some more earlier in the series. Paul O'Connell had a big game – aggressive but disciplined – and Shane Byrne a much happier night at line-out time. He stoically bore the brunt of the criticism after Christchurch, which was, of course, grossly unfair on him. Line-outs are about the calls, the jumpers, the lifters and the thrower. Everything has to work in unison to be successful. No one single person is the cause of a nightmare like the one we endured.

On the subject of line-outs, I never cease to be mystified at rugby's laws and their application. Midway through the first half last night the referee, Jonathan Kaplan, who I thought had an excellent game, suddenly penalized New Zealand twice in quick succession for having too many people in the line-out. No complaints at all from me, but it just seemed very random. One of the key factors in Christchurch two weeks ago – and this was very clear from the match video – was that New Zealand often had too many people in the line-out, an offence according to the letter of the law. I suppose we should have pointed it out forcibly, but when you are playing in a Test match it's just head down, and you rely on the officials to pick these things up. It wasn't deemed an offence then, but it was last night.

Walked on to the pitch after the final whistle to share the moment with the lads, though I felt a bit detached from everything. Wandered around a bit aimlessly in my Lions jacket, blazer and tie, congratulating the New Zealand boys and trying to say the right things to my team, except they weren't 'my team' any more. Their memories aren't my memories. I wasn't there on the pitch putting my body on the line like they did – I was in my jacket in the stand, drinking a cuppa at half-time and enjoying a New Zealand pie and hating every moment of watching, not playing.

Alfie said some very generous words about my captaincy and leadership at the presentation ceremony which were much appreciated and brought a big lump to my throat. I have dedicated myself to being the Lions captain over the last three months and worked harder than at any time in my life. Nothing much at all has gone right. It would be a smidgin easier to take if I had been able to contribute on the field, but it wasn't to be.

Went to the after-match function but didn't feel too great and headed for my cot as soon as it was politic. Possibly a touch of the virus that has been going around, or maybe even the lingering effects of a big night out with Jason Leonard. But probably just tiredness and disappointment and that old habit, when things have gone wrong, of wanting to pull the duvet over your head and wake up to a new world. When I got up this morning and started heading for the airport, some of the lads were still trooping in after a huge night out with the Kiwis. Glad for them, and a little envious – I wanted to mix much more with the All Blacks than has been possible – but also delighted that I felt as sharp as a pin for the never-ending flight home. Auckland, Sydney, Singapore, Heathrow, Dublin. And then number 35. Hope I remembered to cancel the milk.

Monday 11 July, number 35, Dublin

Home at last. The usual stack of mail waiting to be opened. Somebody's done the garden – that's nice. Blue skies, green grass. Couldn't be happier. I will even put up with the micky-taking and smart comments from my mates . . . for a couple of weeks, anyway. They've got to move on as well!

Time to chill out and get this shoulder sorted. Going to see the specialist at Blackrock Clinic tomorrow morning. Want to get things moving quickly – I'm not good when left to fester. Let's get the op done and the rehab under way and start the next day of my rugby life.

Don't feel too bad, all things considered. No hint of jet lag, though I had better not speak too soon. The weather is glorious, so I organized a little barbecue this evening for a few family and friends. Had almost forgotten about my shoulder – it has settled down nicely during the last week in Auckland, perhaps it was the upped alcohol intake – when I went to catch a bread roll I had knocked off the table. Instinctively I reached out with my right hand and was hit with a sharp pain in the shoulder. It was a timely reminder. Let's get this thing opened up and mended.

Tuesday 12 July, number 35

No problems. The diagnosis is exactly the same as down in New Zealand. Booked in for the operation on Friday morning. Action Man Josh Lewsey has been on to say he will send over a CD of all the pics he took because I feature in a fair few of them. Despite my best intentions I was hopeless at snapping away, so anything Josh can provide will be very welcome for the album. He was undoubtedly one of our stand-outs on the tour. He's an incredible athlete – right up there with anybody in the southern hemisphere – and totally committed. Have had a couple of good chats with him and found some of his comments very reassuring. He has been on all sorts of tours with England — the good, the bad and the ugly — and he assures me that this has been as well-organized and happy a tour as any he has been a part of. Like me he was mystified why it just didn't 'happen'. Josh is an independent character and always speaks his mind, and if he wasn't happy about something he would tell you.

Wednesday 13 July, number 35

Went to the building site to see my new house. They already have the plot cleared and the foundations are in place. Thrilled and very proud. We have had to reset our sights for a Christmas completion date, but otherwise it's all good news. Should prove a great diversion over the summer. Glenda can chauffeur me around and we can get all the fittings chosen and ordered.

One of the architects on site was telling me that his local has put up a poster with a picture of Tana: 'Barred for life from these premises'. Another one of the workers came up — a real tough-looking case — and said I should sue for GBH. He was serious.

Since getting back I've been shocked at how much resentment and anger there still is about the incident. When I was down in New Zealand I heard reports from back home, but I had no real idea how huge it had become. You spend most of the time being fed the New Zealand angle and end up not seeing the wood for the trees. I took time out yesterday to read through the papers from the time I was away and there seems to have been more written on the 'incident' than the rest of the tour put together. What I find absolutely staggering is how the Umaga incident has somehow been mixed up and confused with articles on Alastair Campbell – pretty vitriolic attacks – as if they were one and the same. Just don't get it. He could have been living in an ice cave in Alaska or walking on the moon for all the influence he had on this particular story.

The two All Blacks decked me. Shoulder busted. I insisted on making a statement that night and I wanted to turn up to the scheduled 9 a.m. press conference on the Sunday. My decisions. I am a big boy, the 2005 Lions captain. I was bloody annoyed and angry at the time – over the incident itself, over the lack of support from officialdom and the system, and over the attitude of Tana and Keven Mealamu. Time is a great healer; I've pushed everything to the back of my mind now, but at the time I was furious.

Alastair Campbell wasn't a factor in any of that. Nor did he organize or print the protest posters and T-shirts that were around Wellington and Palmerston North the next week, nor did he write the *New Zealand Herald* editorial, nor did he organize the New Zealand press conference when the issue kept coming up, with the Kiwi answers seeming to confuse the issue rather than shed any light.

Going into hospital tomorrow night. Little bit nervous. I've had only one operation before in my life, a knee scope when I was eighteen. It's important everything goes well if I want to achieve my ambition to be playing top-flight rugby at the age of thirty.

Thursday 14 July, Blackrock Clinic, Dublin

All checked in for tomorrow morning's op. It's nicknamed the shark's bite – they open up the shoulder and reset the joint and tighten everything up with sixteen staples so that all the ligaments grow in exactly the right position and the joint returns to full strength. You are left with a fantastic-looking scar, a real beauty apparently, as if a shark has been trying to rip your arm off – hence the name. My permanent memento of New Zealand 2005.

It's been a tough year, and, as the old saying goes, it's only when you stop hitting your head against the brick wall that it begins to hurt. Barry says I should call the book 'the Strife of Brian'. Cheers, Barry! It's all gone badly wrong, though, hasn't it? And after such a promising start in the autumn with Ireland and Leinster. The strange thing is that there was always something to help me bounce back. Six Nations disappointment, but then there was Leinster and the Heineken to dream about. Knocked out of Europe by Leicester, but bring on the Lions. Defeated by the Maori, but there was always the Tests. And now? Well, just getting back playing is a big enough goal. That will keep me going.

Friday 15 July, Blackrock Clinic

Ouch! My shoulder is very painful, like Christchurch all over again. At least this time I can squeeze the morphine drip and get some relief. Everything has gone very well apparently. And I will have a fantastic scar to improve my status with all the hairy-arsed forwards in the changing rooms. The autumn internationals are virtually ruled out, but there is an outside chance of playing for Leinster by Christmas if everything goes well, New Year at the latest. Happy enough with all of that – I'm in no rush and will take exactly as long as it takes to get right – but I hadn't counted on it being so painful when I woke up.

Felt a bit spaced out and woozy when I came around but lying here quietly now watching the Open – extraordinary reception for Jack Nicklaus coming down the eighteenth for the last time. Still playing competitive sport and he's nearly forty years older than me. If you want it bad enough . . .

Trying to plot the way ahead. I'll get out of hospital on Sunday and I will be in a sling for three or four weeks, with my arm strapped close to my chest, before I can do any physio at all. Fancy a proper holiday, for Glenda's sake as much as mine, but can't stand the thought of being in lovely sunny climes for too long trussed up like a turkey. Might nip down to Spain for a week. Otherwise it's time to concentrate on my sister's wedding in August – perhaps I can make myself useful there. No doubt Mum has got a job list she is ticking off by the day.

Keen to get back to number 35 after a few days; recuperating in Clontarf with my folks. I look forward to nipping over to the building site whenever the builders need a yes or no from me. I will probably drive them mad, popping in each day to inspect my new estate! Cooking will be a problem for a while. Just have to eat out more! Can make a fuss of Glenda that way, a bit of a thank-you for driving me around.

Sunday 17 July, Clontarf

Back home with the folks, being waited on hand and foot. Having an operation does have its compensations. Got one eye on the golf – nobody will catch Tiger now, surely – but mostly I am looking through a set of ninety or so photographs by Billy Stickland that will help illustrate this book. Interesting process, sort of compresses and focuses everything that has gone on over the last season. There it all is, on the kitchen table. Feel a bit breathless and knackered just looking at it. Can't decide in my mind whether it has gone quickly or slowly. In some of the early-season photos I've still got the scraggy blond locks and scarcely recognize myself. That seems years ago, another Brian O'Driscoll surely? Mind you, he was on a roll as I recall. Bit like Samson, it all started going wrong when he had his hair cut!

It's been a long and very bumpy ride. Without doubt the toughest year of my rather blessed and protected life, with lots of shade and light, testing situations and crushing personal disappointment. The miles I have travelled – New York, St Barth's, Dublin, Lansdowne Road, Treviso, Bourgoin, Bath, Henley, London, Rome, Warsaw, Spala, Heathrow, Singapore, Sydney, Auckland. Rotorua, Hamilton, New Plymouth – was I in New Plymouth? Yes, that's right, I flew down for the Taranaki game, still feeling dodgy after the scallops – Dunedin, Christchurch, Wellington, Palmerston North and then Auckland again. And then all the way back. Play rugby and travel. Around the world for eighty minutes.

No regrets. In the end nothing worked out at all, but that's the way of the world. I've always loved that John Lennon line – 'Life is what happens when you are busy making plans'.

When you are making plans in sport I've learned to keep them very short term – the next match, the next move, the next tackle. Start thinking too far ahead and you are in dangerous territory. Yes, I still dream of helping Ireland to a Grand Slam and touring South Africa with the 2009 Lions, when I will still be only thirty, but my first goal is simply to get this shoulder healed again. Then comes getting back into the Leinster team in the New Year, and then, God willing, a Six Nations campaign with Ireland.

Funny the things you remember. Belatedly getting that text from Lawrence after the Bay of Plenty match lodges itself in my mind. He is a class act and it was a massive blow – to the squad generally and me personally – missing him after fifteen minutes of the tour. We didn't have much luck, really, nobody seems to comment much on that. To lose Lawrence, myself and Richard Hill in the circumstances that we did – well, that would rock most sides back. We needed everything to go right for us.

Forgot to tell you another little Lawrence story that speaks volumes for the man. Down in the changing rooms at Rotorua, when they were putting his ankle back, looking for the morphine and getting ready to take him to hospital, he suddenly insisted everybody stopped and stripped his Lions shirt off. 'Make sure my opposite number gets this after the match,' he said before they lifted him into the ambulance. I know for a fact that his opposite number – Colin Bourke – was delighted.

I have lived much of the last season under intense media and press spotlight and have tried my best to be helpful and straight-talking. Professional sportsmen make their money because we are public figures and, let's be honest, it is the media and press that make us public figures. We are meshed together for ever more.

But it would be stretching the point to claim that I understand how it all works. There was a stage when I thought I had grasped the principles, but all that was blown sky-high in New Zealand.

Hopefully I can disappear from public view now for six months until I re-emerge as a player. I am hungrier than ever for success on the pitch and, I like to think, more appreciative of those who love and support me, my fantastic family and all my friends, some of whom I haven't even had time to mention in this book.

Let's take a reality check. I live a fantastic life, and my disappointments on the field are absolutely nothing compared with what most people endure in their working lives. I am truly blessed.

Think I will sign off now. I've said everything I want to say about this season. 'Cop it and move on,' as Clive used to say down in New Zealand. Anyway, that sounds like Damo at the front door, no doubt looking to be fed and watered. There are few certainties in life, but you can put your mortgage on his good humour, ravenous appetite and healthy thirst.

Acknowledgements

To Mum and Dad, Geraldine and Frank, for their support and input into this book, and to my sisters Julie and Susan, always encouraging along the way.

To Brendan Gallagher and Michael McLoughlin for literally making things happen.

To Billy Stickland for his superb photographs.

To our friend Justin Paige who started it all and saw it to its fruition.

My special thanks to all who have been part of my life for the past year and in particular all my teammates.

Index

The subheadings are in chronological order.